CW00531413

This book was written …

...after a series of coincidental meetings. Max Brouwer's deeply rooted interest in shooting combined with his profession as photographer gave rise to the photography. Another meeting with Göran Rahm resulted in the text that you now have before you. However, the most important person in this project was Tom Alderin and his God-given talent in drawing out the shooting ability in both game and clay shots on top levels. Finally, we send a thank you to Peter Lönnquist, without whose drive and initiative, this book probably would not have been published.

TABLE OF CONTENTS

Game Shooting the Natural Way

I went game shooting quite frequently in the 1970's and believed I was a good shot, also having some success at clay pigeons. I never reached top flight, far from it, but was pleased with my performance. On the other hand, things could be a little hit-and-miss. Some days went well, others didn't.

I became very interested in shotguns during the mid-1970's. Ranked at the top of course were the best London guns - produced by Holland & Holland James Purdey and Boss, I discovered that an instructor from Holland & Holland, an individual not known to me, had started a shooting school in Sweden at Stora Nyby farm just outside Eskilstuna.

I naturally had read about Lord Ripon and his record for pheasant shooting, over 241,000 pheasants during his lifetime according to the Guinness Book of Records. Guinness himself was no bad shot - reputed to have shot almost 1,000 woodcock during one house party in the grounds at his shooting estate at Ashford Castle. According to legend, the beer king was one of the more successful during this famous shoot. The British, I realised, had a lot to teach me when it came to game shooting.

So I went to Stora Nyby and was greeted by a young man, very properly dressed in a jacket, waistcoat, shirt, tie, plus-fours and chequered socks. He introduced himself as Tom Alderin.

The lesson started with Tom wanting to see how I shot. I hit most of the clay pigeons, shooting incoming, crossing and going away targets. I was quite pleased with myself until Tom said, "There's a couple of things you should think

about. Let me show you."

Tom first showed me how I should stand. Then how I should mount the shotgun, and finally, how I should follow the target. I had never in my life seen anyone handle a shotgun in a more natural and simple way. This observation is still true today.

For many years, Tom was one of Holland & Holland's most sought after instructors - both in London and the United States. He taught for eight weeks each year in America, but in 1986 he put his instructor's shotgun on the shelf for good, or so he thought. After an interlude of several years in the family business, the yearning to teach surfaced once again. When the Swedish Sport Shooting Federation offered him the role of coach for the 1994 Swedish National Shotgun Team, he simply couldn't say no.

During the thirty years that have passed since I first met Tom, he has developed his method to perfection. He calls it "Shooting the Natural Way." The explanations as to "how and why" things are to be done have been refined over the years and have become easier to understand and remember.

What Tom teaches about game shooting in this book actually is nothing more than simply using what you already know and have always known.

GRÄNNA, AUGUST 2006
GÖRAN RAHM

9

Preface

My name is Tom Alderin. I was already fascinated with game shooting by the time I was a teenager. Since then, it has never occurred to me that I would not spend my life doing this.

As all other shots, I asked myself the question: "Why do I sometimes hit the target and other times miss?" This led to the next question: "What factors come together when I hit and what goes wrong when I miss?" To get answers to these questions, I contacted Holland & Holland in London and applied to train as a shooting instructor at their shooting school. This was for several reasons. The primary one was that England, thanks to the three leading weapon manufacturers in London, has had a very long tradition when it comes to training for shooting. Several of the world's best shots have been trained there.

For those who are interested in history, the three London firms, Holland & Holland, James Purdey, and Boss, had already perfected the finest shotgun ever manufactured by the end of the nineteenth century. Their side lock construction is still the ideal for today's weapon manufacturers. Those interested in technique speak of the perfect harmony between the mechanics and weight distribution when it comes to London shotguns. The guns are perfection. Those interested in aesthetics refer to the detailed and beautiful rose-and-scroll engravings on the side plates, box lock plates and trigger guard. These engravings initially were almost hidden by the case hardening and shellac when a gun was first delivered. They were present, eventually appearing when the outer layer began to wear and the metal began to be bared after continual use. In other words, these manufacturers made, and still make, shotguns that became more beautiful the more they are used. Finally, guns speak of the perfect balance and responsiveness. In modern words, one can say that the London firms combined technical perfection with great aesthetic appeal and maximum user friendliness. All this by the end of the 1800's. Now try to convince me that the development has gone forward!

DID I GET ANY ANSWERS TO MY QUESTIONS DURING THE TRAINING?

The answer is both yes and no. Many questions were answered, but the entire time there was an irritating feeling and gnawing in my consciousness. To learn a new manoeuvre, it had to be repeated at least 2,500 times to become automatic. To combine two new movements, each one had to be repeated 2,500 times. In order to then combine these two automatic movements, 2,500 repetitions were further required. We are now up to 7,500 repetitions simply to learn one combination of two movements. As shooting combines many more movements than this, a training program requires endless practice in order to perfect combined movement patterns. There are few persons that have the stamina and strength to force themselves through such

tough training in order to be able to hit a clay pigeon or flying bird with good accuracy.

At the same time as I pondered over training methodology, I realized that human beings do a lot of things without even thinking about them. When we bicycle, for example, we don't think about how we move our hips and the point of gravity or which direction we should turn the handlebars in order to avoid crashing. We carry within ourselves an endless number of mechanized movements that we have trained since birth. It was then that I began to explore whether these movements could be used in connection with shooting and found a simple and certain method that quickly led to clearly better shooting results. I called this method the "natural" method. In contrast with the "training" method, the natural method utilizes what our bodies already know! Through the years as an instructor for Holland & Holland's shooting school in England and in the United States, I have had occasion to develop the method and find explanations for why we human beings move as we do. However, it is difficult to find words for that which is so obvious. Why should one stand so? Why do we miss when we aim? I get such questions all the time from shots that want to improve their shooting technique and from national shooting teams, for which I have been a coach for a number of years. Today I train and coach the Greek national team in Olympic shooting, trap and double trap.

I will attempt to be as honest as I can in this book. It has been published after much encouragement from students and good friends over the years. They have all said, "Summarize your method." My answer has always been, "I am not a man of the pen, I am a shooting instructor." Several of us got together and coincidentally discovered that we could write, edit and design this book. I do not want to tire the reader with this history, but do want to thank the photographer Max Brouwers, Peter Lönnquist, Göran Rahm and Par Löfstedt for their help and commitment during its production.

Therefore, I think it is time to begin with the first lesson.

LESSON ONE
HOW SHOULD I STAND?

Quite often, but not always, the first question I am asked is "How should I stand when I'm shooting?" I usually don't answer this question immediately but instead suggest that the student and I drink a cup of coffee "standing" while the student talks about problems with shooting and expectations for the lessons. After talking a few minutes I usually say, "Look at how you are standing". The student looks questioning to say the least and points out that "this is how I always stand". "Exactly," I usually reply, "As you always stand like that, I think you should continue

to do so even with a shotgun in your hands."

How do 99 out of 100 people stand? Try it yourself. Take a cup of coffee and stand and talk with someone. I'm prepared to bet that you are standing with your feet slightly apart but nevertheless close together. If you shoot right-handed, then you are probably standing with your right foot slightly drawn back. Your left foot is pointing forwards and your right foot is turned slightly outwards. If you shoot left-handed, then you probably are standing with your left foot slightly drawn back and turned outwards. Your right foot is slightly in front and pointing straight forwards. Take a look at your feet and see if I've guessed correctly.

Why do you stand the way you do? You quite simply have learned already from your first steps that this is the most restful and "best" way to stand. Your body has perfect balance with this stance providing the best all around balance.

"The body is lazy, but not stupid," I usually say when talking to a student for the first time. I then note that during the conversation, the student has moved their hips a few centimetres, sometimes to the right, sometimes to the left. This moves the body weight from one leg to the other. Everyone does this without giving it any thought. With the body weight on one leg, the other leg is rested, and vice versa. At the same time, a perfect starting position has been assumed for initiating movement - forwards, backwards or to the side.

This is so obvious that you don't give it any thought. My job as an instructor is to focus your attention on how you move your body and why you do so in one way or another. If we together can bring your well-practised movement patterns to the surface, you will become aware of them, and I can promise that your shooting will improve considerably.

There are two reasons why I have devoted over 30 years in making use of and developing movement patterns you have learned since birth. The first is that the body requires approximately 2,500 repetitions to learn a new movement. The second is that you then have natural answers when you start to ask how and why you should move one way or another. This question is guaranteed to arise at regular intervals! You will hesitate and vacillate many times on the shooting field or the shooting range platform. The answer to how you should act is within you. Ask yourself how you would naturally act when you are not thinking about it.

Developing natural movement patterns and finding natural answers as to how to act in a given situation is the very linchpin of what I call Game Shooting the Natural Way.

If you are shooting in the specialist disciplines such as trap, skeet, sporting, etc., you know from where the target originates. It is also important here to use the natural capacity of the body as far as possible with regard to standing and moving.

Here is an example of naturally acquired ability. The first question that many of my students usually ask when discussing the position of the feet is: "How should I stand if the ground is uneven?" This question answers itself. Move a couple of metres to a level surface where you can stand with stability and comfort. Consider this. If you walk across a ploughed field or after a bird dog in hilly terrain, you always choose the most level and comfortable route. You automatically avoid both bumps and hollows. Your own body has taught you this lesson. It is tiring to go up and down when walking, and it is difficult to shoot from an uncomfortable position, such as sitting in a boat or standing unevenly with one foot high above the other. Always choose the most comfortable position in which to stand, then you'll hit the target.

So now we have reached rule of thumb number one: Even if you have a shotgun in your hands, you must stand as loosely and comfortably as you always stand when having a conversation with someone while holding a cup of coffee.

Is there anything more peaceful than a warm summer night in the Swedish outer archipelago...

...Eider ducks and their young gather in rafts in the straits between the islets. Some evenings they gather by the hundreds. The ducklings squabble while their mothers discuss the events of the day. The drakes are gathered on the side and appear to be discussing life's bigger questions. They are not shy, rather quite the reverse. A drake can quickly take off, suddenly land on a deck with a violent thump, followed by splashy steps. Whatever drew his attention is written in the stars. Perhaps it was a feeling that there was something extra tasty here for supper. With a splash, the drake leaves the boat and reunites with the other gentlemen in the company. These are the summer nights out in the empty Swedish outer archipelago where the warm sea sends tepid breezes to the shore. Autumn and winter are different. Icy,

cutting winds blow on naked skin. Duck decoys rock abandoned in the water. The eiders and golden-eyes are conspicuous by their absence. When they come, they are vigilant and cunning. The slightest movement causes them to go elsewhere. Suddenly, several veer off and come flying into the hide. Incoming shots are the simplest. Straight crossing shots require agility and balance. Those are the ones you remember. Those are the ones everyone talks about. Except my shooting host. He talks about his first eider. The one he did not get when he was ten years old. The weapon was a part of a frame he had cut away from a broken bicycle. He loaded it with black powder and shot in accordance with all the rules of the art. He had found the directions in his dad's book, Hunting, published in 1898. Lacking a hammer mechanism, he had to make due with a fuse of burning driftwood. When the duck approached, unaware of its impending doom, it was time. The bicycle gun exploded violently. The bicycle frame looked like a pile of steel wool. My shooting host got away with only a fright, as did the duck.

LESSON TWO
WHY DOES A SHOTGUN LOOK LIKE IT DOES?

The next time you visit a gun dealer, you should take a closer look at the selection in the gun racks. You will quickly discover that all of the shotguns are very similar. Of course, some have barrels positioned vertically - over and under - is the expression. Others have barrels side by side. Most shotguns today are equipped with a pistol grip. Some with a Prince of Wales grip. A few have a straight handgrip.

If you ignore the pure design features and look at the overall picture, the shotguns are very similar. The question is, why?

The answer is simple. Shotguns have always right from the beginning looked like this. What you see today is a kind of compromise. Or - if you consider all the attempts made and being made - the best compromise. The shotgun is an all-round weapon that enables you to shoot straight upward and even further behind in a confined space. You can use the same shotgun to shoot ground targets or targets out to both sides - both high and low.

Many attempts have been made to generate a different design for a shotgun, but they have simply amounted to time wasted. After a while, every one returns to the original, and the original is not antiquated - it is simply thoroughly tried and tested! Many good shots have commented that the design of the shotgun from as early as the 1800s, after many tests and experiments, is the best for an all-round weapon. The fact that competition shots prefer to adapt the stocks for their own special shooting is quite a different matter. Skeet shooters, for example, have their high and low houses from which the clay pigeons are thrown on the same trajectory each time. This is not the case during game shooting, when the quarry can come from any direction, at any height or any distance!

If you study the shotguns in the illustrations a little closer, you can see that the heel is angled (pitched) in relation to the lower edge of the stock. Underneath, the heel protrudes like

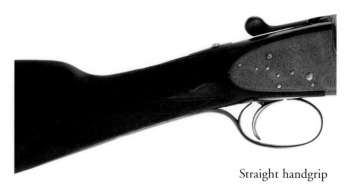

Straight handgrip

Pistol grip

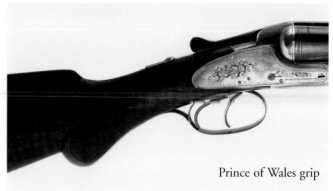

Prince of Wales grip

a tip. The first thing that comes to mind is that this must be wrong. This can't be particularly comfortable if the kick from the recoil is concentrated in one small point against the shoulder. So why has the stock been designed this way? Quite simply because a shotgun is designed to be mounted at an angle of 45-degrees upwards in relation to the upper body! Try this with your own shotgun and you will see. If you aim the barrels at a 45-degree angle up to the ceiling and mount, you will discover how easily and comfortably it falls into place. If you think about it more, you will deduce that 45-degrees is the bisector of a right angle (the line that divides

an angle into two equal halves), in this case, a divisive line directly between a ground target and a target straight above your head.

The question I am often asked is how can you shoot a hare, running on the ground, with a shotgun that must be mounted at a 45-degree angle to the sky. We'll leave this question for the moment and answer it later.

Another question that I am often asked is which type of shotgun is best. My answer is this: "I don't know because we're not the same person." Nonetheless, I normally give advice. If you have decided how much you want to invest in a

shotgun and have a number of models to choose from - choose the model that feels the most comfortable and suits you best. The brand name, how it is engraved or how the barrels are set in relation to each other, is of minor importance. The shotgun that feels best is the one you will

shoot with best and also derive the most pleasure from. Nevertheless, I will give some general advice on the type of gun, as I recommend a shotgun with over and under barrels. You enjoy a more natural line of sight with this type of gun and most people experience it as being easier to "feel" and point with the barrels at the target.

However… I would like to give a word of caution here. When you test mounting a shotgun, it is easy to begin adapting the body to the shotgun. This is wrong! The stock must unconditionally be suited for you!

How do you know what is right or wrong when it comes to the stock? The best way to get an answer to this question is to enlist the help of a shooting instructor. If you don't have anyone who can help, you can try investigating yourself whether a stock suits you. Stand in front of a mirror. Now to begin with, you can establish one thing. Your face is plough-shaped. If you place the palms of your hands against your cheeks and then move them forward, your little fingers will meet in front of your nose.

When you mount the shotgun, your cheek should be in

line with the barrels. Accordingly, you must turn your head slightly - but you must absolutely not tilt it to the side! When you then lift the shotgun up to your shoulder - don't forget that the barrels must be aimed upwards at an angle of 45-degrees - the stock should slide up against your cheek and make contact with it at a height level with the upper row of your teeth. I usually say that when a shotgun suits a person, they should be able to kiss the stock with corner of their mouth. If your eye is centred exactly over the rib, then the fit is fairly acceptable.

However, you must take something into consideration here. To know whether a shotgun is well suited for you, you have to shoot with it. This is inevitable. If you only mount without shooting, your muscles only work statically. When you shoot a moving target, your muscles work dynamically. This is the major difference. My advice, and I repeat this, is that you enlist the help of a shooting instructor before you buy a shotgun. The instructor will be able to see how you are aligned in relation to the target. With the help of a try gun, the instructor can give you your personal stock dimensions and then measure for the shotgun you have decided on. If the dimensions correspond reasonably well and if you decide to buy the shotgun, the gun dealer can then contact a stock maker who can adjust the stock according to the dimensions you have been given. If you do this, you are well equipped then to begin shooting practice in earnest.

To summarise: When you start to shoot, you must choose a shotgun that is well adapted to you individually. If your objective is to be a competent shot, then the shotgun must eventually be adapted according to your own personal stock dimensions - sooner or later.

So now we've reached rule of thumb number two: You must always mount a shotgun at an angle of 45-degrees to your upper body.

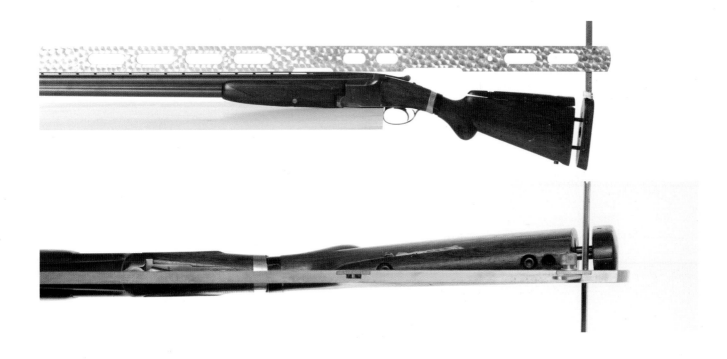

Pigeons are rapacious dining companions...

...living well on arable land. Rapeseed fattens them up, a pure smorgasbord. Mixed crops are pure hors d'oeuvres. In modest numbers, they are a pleasant feature in the landscape. In large flocks, they are a problem to any farmer.

Today, it is a question of culling. The pigeons sit in their flocks and quarrel on the electrical and telephone lines. They appear gorged, resting after breakfast. It is almost as if you could hear the grit grinding the seeds in their gizzards. In some ways, it is like a formal French dinner where the guests have risen to loosen their belts a bit between the third and fourth course. More food is expected. Now it is simply a question of recuperating between courses.

The flankers have positioned themselves round the field and the pigeons are now between the beaters and shots. Hidden under and behind the trees, the tension rises. Two tones from a horn. The beating line moves forward. In the blink of an eye, the prospective feast is transformed into a battlefield. Two, five, eleven, thirty-five pigeons fall in flight followed by slowly descending feathers and down.

It is finished as quickly as it began. Satisfied shots compare their bags while retrievers gather the birds. These are the days one remembers.

LESSON THREE
SAFETY

I have been involved in seventeen incidents where a shotgun has discharged by itself. In fifteen of those cases, it was clearly established that the shotguns had gone off during closing. In two of the cases, I am not certain, but a finger may have been involved in the process.

Seventeen cases during many years and together with an almost innumerable number of shots doesn't sound like very much, but it is seventeen times too many! The likelihood of your

shotgun going off without human involvement is not very great. However, the risk remains and it is a risk you can never ignore!

Nowadays most guns break their shotguns when they are with other guns. This is not just a polite and safe gesture - it is an absolute must! Firstly, a broken shotgun can never go off. Secondly, everyone can see that the cartridges have been removed from the cartridge chambers. It is a bit harder for a person shooting with a semi-automatic. The applicable rule is that the shotgun must be emptied and the bolt drawn back so that everyone can see that the gun is not loaded. If a person approaches with a closed gun, I point out that I feel safer if it is broken. To date as far as I know, no one has taken offence.

In most guns, the safety catch merely blocks the triggers, however, some high quality box locks and most side locks have a secondary safety device called an "intercepting safety sear." Neither of these devices is infallible, any gun with either device can be discharged by an accidental jar or failure of the safety mechanism itself. Therefore, a loaded gun should always be treated as potentially dangerous and only considered totally safe if it can be seen to be unloaded.

As I mentioned earlier, it has become a tradition to break shotguns in the company of other shots. On the other hand, it often is the case that guns close their shotguns and stand them up against a tree or fence, for example. Bearing in mind what has been said about safety catches, it is clear to each and every one of us that the only truly safe way to put a shotgun aside in company is in a broken condition. A closed shotgun that falls over could go off and the charge of shot could hit bystanders. My personal rule is this. The only place I put aside a closed shotgun is in a gun rack.

For these reasons, I am not willing to transport closed shotguns in a gun slip. I have personally chosen to carry my shotgun in a car case with the gun stored in a dismantled condition. The reason for this is as follows: There have been occasions when a gun in a slip has gone off while being removed from a car after transport. Cartridges have been left forgotten in the cartridge chambers. In a number of cases, the accidental shot has led to fatalities. I believe that everyone should be well aware of this. This calls for extra caution. Many people prefer, despite the risks, to protect their gun en route between shooting pegs. Using a gun slip as protection is the simplest solution. If you have a normal, straight slip, you should always as a rule double-check that the gun is really unloaded! A new type of gun slip has recently appeared that I thoroughly recommend. It is a normal slip for composite shotguns, but with the feature that the shotgun can only be inserted if it has been broken!

Many guns load their guns in an unsafe way. Most insert the cartridges and close the gun by lifting up the barrels. When closing, the barrels automatically are aimed parallel to the ground. If a shot were to be discharged in this position, there is a risk that an individual or dog could be hit by the charge of shot.

The best and safest way to close a shotgun is to do the reverse. Instead of lifting the barrels up, lift up the stock with the barrels aimed at the ground. In this position, an accidental shot would be of a significantly less risk to those roundabout. It can be difficult to reload a shotgun in the manner described in certain terrains such as gulleys and hides. The alternative is to aim the barrels upwards during reloading. Accordingly, the basic rule is to avoid at all costs closing the shotgun so that the reloaded gun isn't pointing at anyone else.

A shotgun is handled for the longest period of time while you are standing and waiting at the shooting peg. One good basic rule is to have the barrels aimed towards the ground when shooting ground targets, and aimed upwards when shooting game. Many people allow the shotgun to rest under their arm, gripping the forend with their hand. This is a safe and good way to hold the shotgun, as long as the barrels are aimed towards the ground! What often happens is that the gun loses control of the shotgun when turning around or taking something out of a pocket. In such a situation, it is easy for the gun to lift the barrels so that they suddenly point parallel with the ground instead of being aimed towards it.

During duck shooting, when guns often stand close

together, it is safest to hold the gun straight up with the barrels resting against a shoulder. This perhaps is the most comfortable way to hold a shotgun. It is also safe. A charge of shot straight up into the sky is not likely to hurt anyone.

Naturally, game shooting with bird dogs demands extra caution. It is vital to have a constant watch over both dogs and shooting companions. I normally recommend a posture where the barrels are aimed as good as parallel to the ground, but always so that any accidental shot would travel above the dogs. If you have the barrels aimed straight up in this case, you could easily bring the barrels down to mount for a ground target or a bird taking flight so that they are pointing directly at the dogs. During all walked up shooting or dogging for birds or ground game, it is obvious that you also must take care that shooting companions or beaters don't step in front of the guns.

The issue of safety perhaps has become an obsession for me. As a shooting instructor, I am surrounded by shotguns and firearms all day long. Naturally, no one wants to work with his or her life at risk. Nor do I believe that anyone wants to shoot or practise shooting if there is a risk to his or her own life and health. For me, a good day's shooting or practice is a safe day!

Now I would like to interrupt your reading of the text. If you haven't taken your shotgun from the gun rack yet, please do so now.

First, I would like you to try opening and closing the shotgun in the manner described above and as shown in the illustration. Opening the shotgun with the barrels pointing towards the floor should not present any difficulty. The shotgun opens largely by itself. Closing the gun with the muzzles aimed towards the floor may be more awkward in the beginning until you develop your own style. Personally, I usually twist the shotgun so that is lying along the inside of my right forearm and then the barrels can be closed without raising them from the floor. This way, it is not necessary to lift the barrels to a dangerous position, making it safer. When you try to reload with the barrels aimed at the ceiling, it helps if you have a couple of snap cap cartridges ready. A little practice is required to hold the cartridges in place while closing the gun.

Just one question: What did you do when you took the shotgun from the gun stand? Did you immediately break it or did you turn around with the shotgun resting on your arm? A closed shotgun is always a loaded shotgun! The rule is that as soon as you take a hold of a closed shotgun, it must be broken. This is especially important in situations where you are surrounded by fellow guns.

The same rule applies when you take the shotgun out of the gun slip or from the car. Break it before you turn around and start talking to other guns. Make sure that the barrels are aimed towards the ground or up to the sky.

And while I'm still on the subject.

When and how you prepare the gun for game shooting I discuss later on. But here I'd like to cover what you should do when you have discharged a shot and are about to reload. The shotgun is cocked and you still have one shot left in the cartridge chamber. Many people break the shotgun with its barrels pointing parallel to the ground. Pay attention to the risk that your trigger finger may still be on the trigger when you push over the top lever with your thumb. The result could easily be that your trigger finger braces against the trigger and you accidentally cause a discharge. Make it a rule to always aim the barrels towards the ground before you break the shotgun.

So now we've reached rule of thumb number three: Always break the shotgun when people or dogs are in the vicinity and always break the shotgun when you put it aside against a tree, fence or wall! A broken shotgun is always unloaded. The shotgun must only be closed and ready to fire at shooting stands, on the shooting peg

or in actual shooting situations.

When you have finished the safety training, I would like you to pick out a point on the ceiling moulding that you can mount on. You now know how you should stand. You know that the shotgun is designed to be mounted at an angle of 45-degrees upwards. Try a number of slow mountings first of all and pay attention to what you are doing. Then try to see how fast you can raise the shotgun. What problems do you have? Think this over before you turn the page and continue reading.

Wingspan of about one and a half metres...

... A majestic sight. Even at a distance. Geese in their thousands. Spring or autumn, it makes no difference. The migration north or south is always equally fascinating. A quarter of the world's grey geese are said to breed in Scandinavia. The autumn migration south over southern Sweden through Denmark and Germany is theatre in itself. Plough-shaped formations of hundreds of geese are common. At certain times in the day, the skies are full of them. One often sees thousands of geese at one time.

For farmers, the geese are less charming. Grey geese in large flocks easily cause irreparable harm to crops if not protected. In many places, culling is an absolute necessity. The geese appear to choose the same resting places year after year. Several kilometres away, there are no geese as far as one can see. Where they are gathered, they do so in their hundreds. The purpose of culling is to scare the flocks away from the territory so that they go elsewhere and in smaller groups.

As a shooting guest, one must keep two things in mind. The first is that geese are large and appear to be closer than is the case. Never underestimate the distance. The second is never shoot before you know what you are shooting. Shooting geese requires a good eye. There is an abundance of grey geese. However, rarer species perchance have joined the flock. The Lesser White-Fronted Goose, for example, is a species threatened with extinction. Only a few hundred fertile couples are said to exist in Scandinavia. Shooting this type of goose is not only breaking the law. Landowners and shooting teams never turn a blind eye. As a shooting guest, one becomes a person non grata after such an act.

In the beginning of the 1980's, guns fought to save the Lesser White-Fronted Goose from complete extinction. The geese were captured and newly laid eggs were transferred in cages to barnacle geese that hatched them. The goslings were imprinted on their foster parents. Several weeks before they could fly, the goslings and foster parents were transferred to Artic Scandinavia, the mountain area where the Lesser White-Fronted Goose has always been. When autumn came, the foster parents took the young geese down to the barnacle geese's winter place in Holland. They thrived there and the survival rate was high. The following spring, the young Lesser White-Fronted geese returned with their foster parents to the place where the parents normally mated. The young mountain geese were driven out by the foster parents and returned to the place where they learned to fly. They mated there and had their own young. In the autumn, the Lesser White-Fronted geese flew to the place in Holland where they had wintered the year before.

LESSON FOUR
THE READY POSITION

By now you will have tried mounting several times if you did what I asked in the previous lesson. I assume that you are now standing comfortably, that you are imagining that your shotgun is loaded, and that in your mind's eye, you are standing in your hide with your shotgun over your arm or resting against your shoulder.

Now imagine that you can hear the call of the woodcock or see ducks flying towards you. What do you do?

First, let's visit a gun dealer and see how normal shots who are trying out several different shotguns behave. What do they do?

A fundamental mistake that can often be seen is that they are standing with legs straddled wide apart, as if they were preparing for target practice with a sporting rifle. When adopting the ready position, many people hold the shotgun with the stock at hip height and the barrels pointing diagonally upwards. To mount from such a ready position involves an unnecessarily long lift, making the mounting more difficult. It is then also difficult to gain proper control for aiming the barrels.

What happens when you raise the stock up from hip height to the shoulder is that the shotgun must be rotated around the hand holding the forend. The stock is moved upwards and as a result, the muzzles are in the opposite direction - downwards! If the intention is to shoot at an incoming target, then the muzzles are definitely moving in the wrong direction. The same applies for shooting a target that is ascending or taking flight - the bird naturally starts forwards and upwards away from the gun.

The consequence of such mounting, apart from the fact that the movement is very expansive, is that you lose control of the gun. When the stock reaches the shoulder, much more time is required for correcting the shotgun so that it is aligned correctly and pointing where you want it. In addition, your eye probably will be aligned incorrectly in relation to the rib already from the start.

Now I've told you how not to do it. How should it be done?

Before you mount, you must always adopt a ready position. You must do this irrespective of how much of a hurry you think you are in. The reason is this - if you start correctly, you save a lot of time in the end. You will find the target more quickly. You will be ready to shoot more quickly. In addition, the likelihood that you will hit the target increases considerably.

How to adopt a correct ready position is actually quite obvious. It is important to hold the shotgun so that it can be raised up to your cheek with minimum effort and with the smallest possible movement. You will discover this combination if you hold the shotgun straight forward in relation to your upper body and have the barrels pointing at an angle of 45--degrees upwards in relation to your upper body. The stock should fit under your armpit, level with your chest muscle.

Before proceeding to mounting itself, I would also like to comment as to when it is time to take off the safety catch. According to the old school, the safety catch should be taken off in the same process as raising the shotgun to your shoulder. According to the new school, the safety catch is to be taken off as early as in the ready position. There are many reasons why this is the best method. You can slip the safety catch off in peace and quiet and in a safe manner with your trigger finger remaining on top of the trigger guard. If you slip the safety during the same step as you mount, your trigger finger will then try to move to the trigger during the same step with the risk of an accidental shot as a consequence. If the safety catch is already off in the ready position, you are then ready to shoot when the target appears. If nothing happens, you just need to secure the shotgun again and then resume waiting for the next opportunity to shoot.

After this small digression, it is time to return to the mount. When mounting from a correct ready position, you need only to move the shotgun forward with your front hand while you raise it a couple of decimetres so that the stock slides up and makes contact with your cheek. During this front-aligning movement, your shoulder also moves forward and the heel quite naturally slides into the correct place between your shoulder's outer muscle group and your neck. A small cushion is now formed at your collarbone against which the heel can rest. This is a very small movement, so you also have complete control over the gun while you "sense" exactly where the barrels are pointing! You don't need to check. You know!

Whether you have all the time in the world or think you are in a hurry because the target suddenly appears, it is that small moment - the fraction of a second - that you need to adopt the ready position that is so important for the rest of the procedure. You take off the safety catch. That takes perhaps one-tenth of a second, and you start to adjust your body and actively meet the target so that you can directly start to swing when the shotgun is pressed against your shoulder.

I shall return to this process of adjusting your body and meeting the target again and again later on in the book.

Now it's time for a dry run!

Position yourself so that you have the ceiling moulding at a 45-degree angle above your head. Look at one point, the head of a nail or a paint bubble that you can shoot at. Adopt the ready position and try several mountings on this point.

Start by mounting as quickly as you can several times. Then do the same thing, exactly as I described above and as slowly as you possible can. Think a little about the difference between fast and slow mounting before you turn the page. I believe that we will arrive at the same conclusion. If you are in a hurry, you lose time! Take it easy, and you gain time!

Now to rule of thumb number four: Always adopt the same ready position however much of a hurry you believe you are in. The alternative is to learn to mount from an infinite number of different positions.

Those who claim that they understand the English language lie...

... After having consulted with the Concise Oxford Dictionary, I maintain that not even Englishmen know what their neighbours are talking about. Take simply the word "game". Are they talking about wild animals, meat, past-times, play, competition, good sportsmanship or what? I don't even dare begin with the word "shoot." It can mean anything. Wounding someone, an extension, a branch, rapids, throwing, and more and more. It's not strange that one can converse for hours with an Englishman in the belief of complete agreement. Everyone agrees, despite the fact that they are speaking in some cases of wildly different things.

One phrase, however, is unambiguous. Family shoot! It is game shooting, but not game shooting. It is serious, but not serious. It is shooting, but not shooting. It is a folk festival. Clear and simple. The families in the countryside gather here. Children, youths and adults. Some with dogs. Others without. Some with walking sticks. Some with diverse horns of different sizes. Most with picnic baskets. The shooting can go as it wants. It is only a little part of something as old as mankind. Gathering. Fellowship. Roots. Equality. A family shoot quite simply is a splendid day together with friends and acquaintances. Some are equipped with shotguns in order to contribute by word and deed to the evening's meal.

LESSON FIVE
MOUNTING

Did you try mounting several times as I asked in the previous lesson? If so, you probably discovered that you acted slightly differently when you mounted quickly compared to when you mounted as slowly as you could.

When you mounted slowly, I imagine that you raised the shotgun up so that the stock rested correctly against your shoulder - against the small cushion that forms over your collarbone between your shoulder muscles and neck. At the same time, I imagine you turned your head slightly so that your cheek touched the comb. This way, your eye lined up with the rib. Had you shot against the point on which you had focused, you would have hit it. If you did this exactly, you performed a perfect mount, almost. But we'll get back to this.

Now try to mount again several times.

Of course, I don't know how you are holding the shotgun when you mount. But I imagine that your eye is aligned slightly differently each time and that you need to slightly adjust it to align it correctly. You are now perfectly entitled to ask the same question that I'm always asked by my new students: "Where should the comb press against my cheek?" My answer is always the same: The comb should meet your cheek exactly at a height level with, and parallel to, the upper row of your teeth. Your head should only be turned - not tilted - and the contact should be such that you can kiss the stock with corner of your mouth. (Close-up of face - stock).

Try again. If your shotgun is equipped with a standard

stock and you think it mounts well, then I imagine your eye is now aligned "exactly" in line with the rib. However, you will quickly discover that it is not quite exactly centred. The position of your eye varies slightly. At one time, it can be slightly to the left, and at another, slightly to the right. Sometimes a little higher, sometimes a little lower. Don't worry about that today! Your eye will be aligned in all certainty within

what I call the "acceptable margin of error." You won't get a perfect bull's-eye when you shoot - but you will get a hit! And this is what is most important right now.

However! You should always bear in mind that it is the stock that aims - never you! (See fitting the stock, Lesson Two and Appendix 1). You can tolerate a minor misalignment for a certain amount of time, as a beginner never mounts exactly the same each time. Adjusting the stock according to your own exact personal dimensions straight away is not necessary. You can start thinking about adjusting the stock when you have begun finding your feet, providing that the basic fit is correct. If not, you should enlist the help of a shooting instructor. This is a very good investment viewed in relation to other costs. Shooting costs a lot of money, there are costs for transport, clothes and equipment, and guns are expensive. Seen from this perspective, the checking of stock dimensions and an investment in several shooting lessons are trifling sums, especially as this minimal investment is guaranteed to increase your hit percentage and accordingly, give you a higher return from this great sport.

Now let us summarise mounting up to this point. You mount the shotgun at a 45-degree angle to your upper body. You push the shotgun forward and up with your front hand, the hand holding the forend. The heel rests against the small cushion formed over your collarbone between your shoulder muscle and neck. The comb rests against your cheek (without you tilting your head) at a height and parallel with the upper row of your teeth. If you fulfil these criteria each time you mount, then the barrels will also point in the same direction as you are looking!

The whole point of this training is that you should both observe and convince yourself that this really is the way. The idea of the exercise is to reinforce your conviction, so that you do not waver in your belief for even one second. This is one of the linchpins for successful game shooting.

Now to rule of thumb number five: From this moment on, talking about "resting the shotgun against the shoulder" is taboo. From now on, we only talk about raising the shotgun to the cheek!

That was a short and uneventful lesson. Although perhaps the most important in the whole book! This is an exercise that you should repeat as often as possible. Preferably daily. When the mount is perfect, the raising of the shotgun and the small turn of your head are changed into a single coordinated movement. You don't do one first and then the next, you do everything at the same time.

I apologise for this long introduction. I imagine that you are expecting to learn how to swing and the lead distance with a flying bird in order to successfully hit the target. It's coming, I promise, but first I must impose upon your patience for a few more lessons.

One more thing. When you have practised mounting for a while, your arms will probably tire. The shotgun weighs up to three and a half kilograms. If you have swung as well, then it is conceivable that the wrist of the front hand is tired. If this is the case, you are then making another common mistake, but I'll return to this in the next lesson.

Shooting clay pigeons is a pleasure...

... But you must be careful. Clay pigeons are inanimate objects. In the joy of pure shooting, one can become over-confident and begin to be careless. With clay pigeons, it harms no one. Possibly one's own ego. During a shoot, out in reality, the situation is different. The target is a bird of flesh and blood. Respecting wildlife and the nature we live in is the hallmark of a genuine hunter. Carelessness is a taboo. A gun who is well prepared and refrains from making impossible shots is always a welcome shooting guest.

GRIPPING THE FOREND

This is a small supplement to the first lesson on mounting. At this point, I would like you to start playing ball with an orange, apple or preferably, a tennis ball. Throw it straight up with one hand and catch it with the same hand. Do this several times and watch your hand. Without thinking about it, you hold your hand so that it becomes a linear extension of your forearm. As soon as you got your first ball, your body learned that this was the best and easiest way for you to hold your hand when you played ball or lifted something.

Now take your shotgun and hold out the hand you use to grip the forend, the front hand. Lay the forend on your hand. If you are holding your hand in the same way as when you played ball, the forend inevitably will be diagonal in the palm of your hand - from your wrist and straight over the lower part of your forefinger. If you hold the forend this way when you mount, you will also raise the shotgun in the way your body wants and is used to. The mistake many people make is that they grip the forend in the same way as they grasp an object such as a crowbar, for example. They have the forend across their hand. This way naturally provides a firm grip, but it is not a question here of holding the shotgun firmly, it should just simply rest in your hand.

Before we continue, I would also like to comment on the grip with the hand holding the small of the stock. This grip should also be loose and during mounting, your hand should just follow along and be moved parallel in relation to the front

hand holding the forend and leading the mounting. The small cushion of muscle on the trigger finger's furthest joint should rest in contact with the trigger.

Now back to the front hand.

If you try to lay the forend across your hand, you have to angle it in relation to your forearm when you mount. If you grasp the forend in this way, you lock several of the muscles in your forearm and shoulder. Instead of your hand lifting the shotgun gently and elegantly, these muscles offer resistance. If you swing with this grip, the resistance from these muscles will then brake the swing at quite an early stage, and this is not particularly beneficial for hitting the target.

A simple mnemonic rule: The hand in which the forend rests is always the hand that leads the swing!!! Never forget this.

When you have the correct grip on the forend, your forefinger will be in line with the barrels. It will be aligned either along the lower edge of the forend or, as I prefer, with the forend over your middle and ring fingers so that it just touches your little finger with the forefinger positioned at the side of the forend, but so that it still points in line with the barrels. This grip has two advantages. It is the most

comfortable and you point towards the mounting point (I don't wish to use the term "aiming point" because if you aim in this way, you inevitably will miss a moving target). You have always known how to point towards a particular spot. You can also start to point with your arms hanging straight down, raise your arms then follow a bird flying past with a very high degree of precision. Why, and how it works, I'll return to eventually.

There is one more thing I would like you to do while you are still playing ball. I'm prepared to bet that you always follow the ball with your eyes when you throw it up and catching it. Now try watching your hand instead. You perhaps can manage to catch the ball if you throw it up simply a few decimetres, but if you throw it higher, there's a good chance that you won't be able to catch it. I only want you to make a note of this now, as I will also return to this later on.

So it's time for rule of thumb number six: The hand holding the forend should be an extension of your forearm and the forend accordingly should be held diagonally across the palm of your hand.

Summer. Woodcock fly...

Their song is unmistakable. The shotgun is taken on the evening walk. Mostly out of old habit. Here in the late summer twilight, thoughts drift. Captured by the wood ants swarming around an anthill. Chaos without comparison. But appearances are deceiving. If you look closely, you discover organization. Each individual ant appears to know its destination and task. The instincts controlling this are incomprehensible. Of course, yes! The woodcock. It flew by while thoughts wandered in a different direction. The dog barks reproachingly. In his world, retrieving is everything. Ants … ah, what does he care for such small creatures.

LESSON SEVEN
THE INCREDIBLE BRAIN

I would now like you to enlist the assistance of a spouse or shooting companion for this little experiment.

Stand facing each other. Ask your partner to hold up a cartridge with two fingers a bit out to the side. However, no further than you can reach. Stand up straight with your arms hanging at your sides. Then take the cartridge.

Simple, isn't it? Do the same thing again, though this time with your arms bent. Just as simple, isn't it? Do the same thing again but start with your hand somewhere else. Still just as simple, isn't it?

Now repeat the procedure and feel how your hand moves. Do this without taking your eyes off the cartridge!!! You will discover something quite fantastic. Your hand is moving in a straight line, that is the shortest route from its starting point to the cartridge. It doesn't matter where your hand was when you started. You may of course also be surprised that you managed to take the cartridge without your hand even touching your partner's hand. This is

indicative of fantastic programming. What is so remarkable about this? Two levers control the movement of the hand. The upper arm moves in a semicircle and the forearm moves at a right angle in relation to the upper arm. Equally confounding is that the hand takes the shortest route from its starting point to the cartridge.

What controls your hand? That's the question. Well, now we have reached what is absolutely the most important when shooting moving targets (incidentally, this is also as true for ball sports). It is your eye that controls your hand. When you focus on something, your vision controls your brain, which in turn starts to send signals to your fine motor control muscles. These in turn take control of the larger muscles also included in the fine motor control system. All of these signals mean that the levers, the hand and fingers cooperate in an incredible way, and this without you ever even thinking about it in your entire life! You don't think about it because that's what you've done your whole life, from the moment you discovered a mobile hanging and swinging in front of you when you lay in your crib.

No one really knows in detail how this works. One thing experts agree upon, however, is that the large muscles remember movements and learn to repeat them automatically. We can simply verify that the brain consists of more than tens of billions of cells and also that each individual cell can transmit or receive 200 signals per second. So we are talking about an extremely quick broadband. It has been asserted that the human brain has a greater signal capacity than all the computers in the world - connected together! I don't know whether this is true, but the capacity of the brain is astonishing.

Now do the above exercise again and think about how many muscles you use to take the cartridge. If you guess that

it takes around fifty muscles, then you guessed right. This is approximately as many as are activated when you make this automatic movement with your hand.

You should remember the lesson of this little experiment for as long as you continue to shoot and hunt. The eye and focus control the fine motor control which in turn always ensures that you move the shortest route from one point to another using the large body muscles included in the fine motor control system. In a larger context - when you swing the shotgun during shooting - your eye and focus control the fine motor control so that the barrels always take the shortest route from the starting point to the target. This is precisely what we want to achieve when we mount behind a moving target to swing through with it!

Rule of thumb number seven - Never let the target out of your sight when shooting. It is your eye and focus on the target that controls your movement!!!!
"Game Shooting the Natural Way"

Still nights at the lake.

...Mallards come flying in from their feeding places out in the arable landscape to their breeding places on the edge of the water. When the time, wind and flight are right, the lake issues an invitation to a couple of good shooting evenings. However, not tonight. A moose with her calves cools off with a dip in the sea. From another direction, the bull comes to join them. The time for mating approaches and the courtship has begun.

Breast of wild duck, stuffed with cep mushrooms

INGREDIENTS FOR 4 PORTIONS

4 x wild duck breasts
4 dl sherry
3 x shallots
approx. 70g frozen or fresh cep mushrooms
approx. 50 g Philadelphia cheese
4 dl chicken stock
Butter
Salt and pepper
Maizena or arrowroot

COOKING PROCESS

Finely chop half of the shallots and the cep mushrooms and fry together in a saucepan. Allow them to simmer together with a little chicken stock.

Mix these ingredients in a food processor until creamy
Mix in a little Philadelphia. Allow to cool.

Cut the breasts in the centre and fill with the mushroom cream
Then tie the breasts together with twine.
Add salt and pepper and brown the breasts in a frying pan.
Transfer the breasts to an oven plate.
Put the plate in the oven at 150 degrees for 10-12 minutes (the breasts should be pink inside)

Pour away the fat in the frying pan and then fry the remainder of the chopped shallots.
Simmer together with the remainder of the chicken stock and the sherry.

Thicken to a sauce and strain over the breasts.
Serve with hot oven roasted potatoes.

LESSON EIGHT
THE TREACHEROUS BRAIN

When you start to realise just how fantastic the brain is, you should also bear in mind that the brain is also a truly cunning piece of work.

Now repeat what you did in the previous lesson. Ask your partner to hold the cartridge up so that you can take it, but this time close your eyes and try to take it without knowing where it is! I assume that this also went well, but what exactly happened?

First and foremost - your hand didn't take the shortest route to the target, did it? You fumbled your way forward. This time only your brain had control. You calculated that you had to fumble to the right and left, up and down, until your fingers bumped into the case. Or perhaps you first bumped into your partner's outstretched hand.

Do the same thing once more and make a note of how many muscles you use.

What did you deduce? If you guessed that you used half as many muscles compared with when you focused with your eyes on the case, then you guessed right.

The big muscles are controlled by the will. It is your will - that is, the part of your brain connected to your logic - that controlled your hand. This works very well if you are moving something heavy. You and your partner, for example, should be able to take hold of a large stone from your respective sides, count "one-two-three", and then lift it.

Now to go back to the previous lesson. There we agreed that your eye and focus and the fine motor control muscles cooperate so that you move an object the shortest route from one point to another. You do this with the help of a "built-in" sense that you have developed from the day you were born. You do it without any conscious assistance at all!

After trying to take hold of the cartridge with your eyes closed, you have seen for yourself that when your brain and intellect take control, your fine motor control is disconnected. You are correcting your positioning the entire time with the help of your logic. Eventually you will get it right, but the path

is both long and tortuous.

Now you object! Despite everything, a shotgun weighs around 3.5 kilograms. It is heavy, and the fine motor control muscles are not sufficiently strong to swing it. It requires significant strength both to lift and swing a shotgun.

I accept your objection. But then, you have forgotten that your eye and focus, your fine control muscles and large muscles all cooperate. The difference, when you are focusing on the target, is that your eye and focus and fine motor control muscles take command and also control your body's large muscles. Your eye and fine motor control hold the conductor's baton and your large muscles follow their directions.

I think I will digress here to illustrate the connections we have so far discussed.

I usually give beginners four basic instructions before they're allowed to shoot. One - mount on a point behind a clay pigeon. Two - focus on the clay pigeon the entire time. Three - swing the shotgun through and past the target. Four - pull the trigger precisely when the barrels pass the clay pigeon and without stopping the swing through. This works - the student shatters the clay pigeon. The hit perhaps is not perfect, but the clay pigeon breaks.

Now I usually allow the student to continue shooting - and suddenly - after five, seven or ten shots, the student starts to miss. Why?

This is where the treacherous brain enters. It tells the student, "You and I can do this now. We'll work together so that we score perfect bull's-eyes with every shot. Now we'll turn the clay pigeons into powder."

What's happening? Well, the student naturally stops focusing on the clay pigeon, what I call "defocusing," and starts aiming instead. The fine motor control that should move the barrels the shortest route from the mounting point up to and past the clay pigeon is disconnected. The brain and big muscles take over and the swing stops. The trigger finger does its job - but as the swing stops, the charge of shot often passes far behind the clay pigeon.

This is a problem that affects everyone - beginners and experienced competition shots alike. And what happens when you start to miss? You lose self-confidence! You doubt yourself. You doubt your eye and you doubt your fine motor control. You doubt Mr. Tom Alderin! So now the brain gets seriously involved in the process, thinking and working out what went wrong, needing to correct the mistakes, and then the barrels stop swinging!

Accordingly, when a beginner has missed a couple of clay pigeons, we start again from the beginning. The beginner is given exactly the same instructions as previously, but with the request - Don't aim! The hits then come as certainly as a letter in the post. I can in confidence disclose here that a top shot who has poor hits or misses is given exactly the same instructions.

After this lesson, you can surely understand why I have so stubbornly encouraged you to practise standing correctly, to practise holding the shotgun correctly, to practise adopting the correct ready position and to practise mounting on a point while you focus on the target the entire time. The more you practise, the more convinced you will be that the barrels are pointing in the direction you are looking without you needing to check!

Of course, this sounds easy. The question is only how you are looking and what you should look at. I'll return to this in Lesson Eleven. At the moment, you need only to drum in the following rule of thumb. No doubt you've already worked out what it is: ALWAYS FOCUS ON THE TARGET! Never focus away from the target. Trust that the barrels are pointing in the direction they should be and are taking the direct route from the mounting point up to and past the target.

You will now finally get an answer to the question you probably were asking right from the first lesson - How large a lead do I need to hit a moving target?

Rule of thumb number eight - Always focus on the target!!!

Positioned in a duck blind...

...Hidden at the bottom of a ditch. Well-shielded and dressed in camouflage. Dandelions grow profusely here. Those small yellow flowers. Heartily hated by some. As loved by others. All depending upon your view. For many, dandelions are weeds that destroy lawns and are to be exterminated. For others, they are beautiful, living flowers. A type of yellow-gold miniature iris. A dichotomy of views similar to that of predators and prey. For those who see hunting as exploiting natural resources, predators are thoroughly hated. For those who see the hunt as a natural part of a functioning ecosystem, it is an exhilarating experience when studied in the wild. Eagles, owls, foxes, and badgers. All have found their niche to survive. It would be a travesty to disturb this balance.

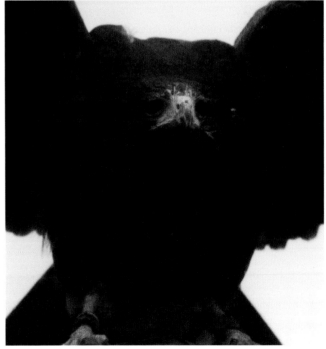

LESSON NINE
UTILIZING THE LAW OF INERTIA

Now it's time to take a look at what happens in practice when you fire at game.

You have, of course, tried to mount several times on a point on the ceiling moulding - perhaps in the corner - while you focused on a point further forward along the moulding. Naturally, you have also tried to swing the shotgun from the corner and all along the ceiling moulding past the point you are focusing on. You have probably also been able to observe that the muzzles very kindly follow the moulding without you needing to control the barrels, in other words, aim.

If you focus in the same way on a clay pigeon or a bird in flight, the barrels will follow the straight line from the mounting point behind the bird, forward and past it. Your fine motor control ensures first of all that the muzzles follow the bird's line of flight. If you don't slow your swing down but continue past the bird, your fine motor control will ensure that the muzzles continue along the line on which the bird is flying! If you pull the trigger precisely when the muzzles pass the bird, you will hit the target!

WHY? FIRST, A SMALL DIGRESSION.

Many students ask me how large a lead is required to hit the target. My answer has been the same for more than thirty years now - I have no idea. If I started to think about it, I certainly would miss!

To see how this works in practice, you should ask your partner to stand behind you. You should be standing several metres from the living room window and imagine you are following the flight of a bird. Precisely when the barrels pass the window frame, pull the trigger. So where did it click? Your partner will answer that it clicked when the muzzles had long passed the frame.

What happens is exactly that which happens in the nursery rhyme, the old lady who swallowed a spider to catch a bird, and swallowed the bird to catch the cat, swallowed the cat to catch the dog, etc.

- The eye tells the brain to shoot.
- The brain tells the spinal cord to shoot.
- The spinal cord tells the trigger finger to shoot.
- The trigger finger squeezes.
- The pressure releases the tumbler.
- The tumbler strikes the firing pin.
- The firing pin strikes the percussion cap.
- The percussion cap ignites the charge.
- The charge starts to burn and becomes gaseous.
- The gas pressure forces the shot charge through the bore...

...and only then is the charge of shot en route to the target.

While all this is in progress, you managed to swing the shotgun past the target. When the charge of shot finally exits the bore, the muzzles are pointing far ahead of the target. This is the process I call the law of inertia, and this is what you should rely on in the future.

Now continue with the practice dry run with your partner as supervisor. Try to swing very slowly - it clicks slightly after the window frame. Then swing more quickly. You will notice that it clicks a lot further forward in the swing. This is the way in which the law of inertia works in combination with an accelerating swing.

This works as follows when shooting against a moving target: If you are shooting a fast bird, you must swing more quickly and the law of inertia then ensures that the shot is fired when the barrels are pointing a long way in front of the bird. If you are shooting a slow target, then you swing more slowly and the lead automatically is accordingly less.

Believe it or not, thanks to the law of inertia, the lead actually takes care of itself! What you must practise - and of course this must be on a shooting field - is finding your own swing speed or timing, as it is called. Timing means time required! Timing is governed by a type of built-in clock that we're all equipped with - right from birth.

Now remember to always take the same length of time - have the same timing - from when you mount behind a bird to when the muzzles pass it. The swing speed is then determined by how quickly the bird is flying!

For the sake of simplicity, let's assume that your timing is barely one second.

The bird is flying quickly, so you have to swing quickly in order for the muzzles to catch up in less than one second. When you pull the trigger and the law of inertia has been invoked, i.e. when the shot actually fires, the barrels are aimed a long way in front of the bird. Naturally, this presupposes that you do not stop the swing but swing through and past the target with uninterrupted acceleration. This is an absolute must! The lead accordingly has regulated itself. If the bird is flying slowly, then you must swing more slowly. Your timing indicates that it should take barely one second to swing the barrels from the mounting point, up to and through the target. When you pull the trigger, the lead accordingly will be reduced. (I hope that you notice this yourself by means of the exercises against the window frame.) Forget any thoughts about trying to calculate the lead in metres. Do not think of the lead at all! Instead, trust your timing and the law of inertia. In order to quickly find your individual timing, I recommend that you take several shooting lessons from an experienced instructor.

Another question that sometimes arises is how large a lead there should be for different shooting distances. I answer this the same as before: I have no idea. Neither you nor I know how far it is to the target. Nor do we know how quickly the target is moving. The question consequently is purely academic.

The next lesson is about ball sports.

Now for rule of thumb number nine - Never try to calculate the lead in metres. You know neither how fast the bird is flying nor how far away it is: Instead, let your body and eye sense the movement!

Two rivers form the hub in a wheel, the author...

...Artur Lundkvist describes in one of his poetry collections. And the rivers are never given the wrong names. Time, events and the experiences of mankind generate names that fit them like a hand in a glove. Neither can a brook have a wrong name. Here it is not a question of a large flow of water. But the stream has a deaf sound. As thunder at a distance. And the little island in the middle of the stream below the end of the rapids invites rest for tired legs. Carved out in the ravine in the stream and well hidden by bushes, it is no farther from the shore than simply a step over. Here, in the midst of the stillness, a moose family sometimes walks by. Soundless, almost ghostlike. Below the island a tributary contributes with more water. Colder, rich in minerals and with a watering place for hoofed wildlife upstream. Artur Lundkvist sees the world from a global perspective. In his eternally turning water wheel, the rivers are called the Min and Yangtze. Here, seen from a considerably more narrow perspective, Thunder Brook and Cloven Furrow create the eternally turning water wheel. The island's name is equally self-evident. The locals refer to it as "Ghost Island."

LESSON TEN
THE IMPORTANCE OF A SMOOTHLY ACCELERATING SWING

I commented in Lesson Six that game shooting has certain similarities to ball sports. Watch a tennis player. He focuses on the ball as it approaches, moves the racket far behind his back, strikes the ball and only finishes the stroke when the racket is on the other side of his body. At the back of the back swing, the movement stops for a moment and from there, a smoothly accelerating front swing starts that strikes the ball at full power, stopped only after a full rotation.

Watch a golfer. He does things the same way. He focuses on the ball at his feet. He lifts the club upwards and backwards so that the shaft is behind his back. A smooth acceleration forwards starts there, with the head of the club hitting through the ball at full force. The swing doesn't finish until the club head has revolved around the player for more than a full rotation. During the entire swing, his focus is only on the ball. If you watch carefully, you will notice that a good golfer doesn't even raise his eyes when he hits the ball. He doesn't look up until well after the ball has been struck.

Focus on the ball is the first key concept in ball sports. Timing is the other.

A tennis player can lob a soft shot. When he does this, he doesn't reach as far back with the racket as when striking with full force. A golfer can hit 25, 40, 65 or 125 metres with the same club. If he wants to hit a 25-metre stroke, he doesn't move the club back as far. If he wants to hit 125 metres, he hits with a full swing.

When a golfer controls the swing speed, we talk about timing. Timing, as I said in the previous lesson, is a type of built-in clock that we all are gifted with. Neither tennis players nor golfers need to think in order to hit the ball exactly as hard or as long as they want. By training, the big muscles have learned how much they need to exert, and it is in the big muscles where the built-in clock is located. It is there where

you can find the "swing memory" or timing.

The similarity between shooting and ball games is actually quite striking. Imagine the barrels are the handle of a racket. Then imagine that the line between the barrels and the bird is the shaft, and finally that the charge of shot is the sweet spot. Translated into tennis terms, you raise the shotgun-racket behind the target and hit forwards and through. You fire exactly when the barrels are passing the target and you connect the sweet spot in the form of a charge of shot.

When you use a shotgun as a racket, the stumbling block is that you doubt whether shooting could be so simple. You don't dare believe that it is as easy to hit a flying bird as it is to hit a flying ball with a tennis racket!

WHY IS THIS SO?

As soon as you mount, your brain wants to be involved and check that the barrels really are aimed at the point you want them to be. You aim, that is to say you look at the racket instead of the ball. Why would you hit a clay pigeon when a tennis player invariably misses the ball if he takes his eyes off of it and looks at his racket instead?

When the shotgun-racket should fell the bird, the brain is there again. It wants to check that the barrels really are aimed exactly at the bird and not over or under. You aim. That is to say you look at the racket instead of the ball. If a tennis player misses the ball when he acts in this way, why should you hit a clay pigeon?

After this little digression into the world of ball sports, you hopefully will understand the importance of carrying out the exercises I suggested in Lesson Five. You must convince yourself that when the stock is correctly aligned, the barrels then point to where you are looking, without you needing to check. The fact is that you can point with the barrels at a fixed point while you are focusing on something completely different. The reason why is partially explained here, with the rest of the answer given in the next lesson.

I covered the areas of lead, the law of inertia and timing in the previous lesson. We'll take a look at them also from a ball sport perspective.

Your opponent on the tennis court doesn't shout: "Now I am hitting the ball at a 32-degree angle in relation to the court's centre line and at a speed of 87 km/h." The player registers the trajectory and speed of the ball instinctively, moves to the right place at the right time and returns the ball. All this takes place without any thought or looking at anything other than the ball even for a split second.

A football player doesn't shout to a team-mate who has found a free area in the opponent's penalty area: "Now I am making a kick that is 416 centimetres up above the ground that will bounce 185 centimetres in front of your left foot if you move towards the right goalpost at a speed of 21 km/h." The football player focuses on the ball and makes a kick that ends up in front of the feet of his team-mate.

HOW DO THESE LAST EXAMPLES ACTUALLY WORK?

Despite the football player's constant concentration on the ball, he nevertheless registers when a team-mate is free, the direction in which he is moving, and where the ball should be so that his team-mate can make a shot. This is what is called an "eye" for the game.

Team sports are an excellent example of how we human beings can focus on an object while we both perceive and control actions in our periphery. Which means that it now is time to review how the eye works.

Rule of thumb number ten - To apply a well-rehearsed parallel as to focusing and swinging, you can consider the shotgun as the shaft of a tennis racket and the bird as a ball. Focus on the bird, raise the racket and hit it with a smoothly accelerating movement.

Common snipes are difficult birds...

... Shooting a common snipe taking off in a bog without a dog is clearly one of game shooting's true tests of agility. The birds almost always take flight in pairs and at full speed at the first flap of their wings. They have a habit of crossing each other's paths. Shooting pairs of birds is one of the hardest things there is. For everyone except the old timers who sit in the pub telling shooting tall-tales to each other. Many listeners would really be convinced that these old boys truly are specialists in killing two birds with one shot, shooting at the exact moment that the common snipes' flight paths' cross. In their world, it is the single shot hitting both birds that matters. We others have to be satisfied with one bird. Often with both barrels, in other words, a second barrel kill.

LESSON ELEVEN
FOCUS, GOOD VISION, VISUAL MEMORY AND MOTION VISION

Some attention has been devoted so far to vision and focus, but how do we really see?

Provided you are not focusing on anything in particular and looking around with a "wide vision" that also includes peripheral motion vision, you have a field of vision approaching 180-degrees. You can see different objects and ground level formations relatively sharply in the centre of this field of vision. Further out in the periphery, you can detect movement. When you "instinctively feel" that there is a deer far out to the right or left and then look there, this isn't because of any intuitive ability. The explanation is rather that the animal moved. What your motion vision exactly perceived

was a movement and you looked instinctively in that direction.

It is the wide vision and motion vision that have saved us human beings from dire straits as long as we have existed. Without the help of motion vision, we could scarcely drive a car without incident.

Focus is the direct opposite of motion vision. According to all available research, you can focus on an area that is 0.2 mm2. That's right, square millimetres, you read this correctly. You can actually verify this here and now. Try focusing on the first "m" in the term "square millimetre." You can see three of four letters around the "m" quite well. The rest of the term is

blurred and you can hardly read what is there. If you now stop focusing on the "m" and look across the entire term, you can read it without difficulty. If you think this over a little, you will come to the conclusion that in reality, you are equipped with four different types of vision:

1. Focus;
2. "Good vision" (my term for the inner field of vision where you see the three or four letters around the "m" while focusing on the "m");
3. Wide vision with visual memory;* and
4. Motion vision.

I know that the above exercise is a little tricky; focusing actually requires practice. What probably happens is that while you focus on the "m", you suddenly can read the entire term "square millimetre". You then have stopped focusing on the "m" and are looking with wide vision. This often happens during actual shooting, especially in the beginning. The student stops focusing on the front of the target and looks with wide vision. You already know what happens then from having read Lesson Seven. There is a major risk that your fine motor control becomes disconnected, which has a negative effect on the swing. This often results in a miss or in the best case, a very poor hit.

Back to focusing and the small area of 0.2 millimetres squared. When you focus on a bird or clay pigeon 20 metres away, you have no difficulty in focusing on the bird's beak or the front edge of the clay pigeon. However, some practice is required to avoid "defocusing."

You now are going to do something that is absolutely forbidden in a gun context. Break the shotgun so that both you and your partner can see that no cartridges are in the cartridge chambers. When this is done, ask your partner to stand approximately one metre in front of the muzzles and hold a cartridge up in front of them. Focus on a small point on the

cartridge, a letter or the front edge of the bottom of the cartridge, and then ask your partner to slowly move it straight around to the side. Maintain focus on the cartridge without following with the barrels. Notice that you "sense" exactly where the barrels are pointing without needing to check. Despite the fact that you are focusing on a small point on the cartridge, you can still see the barrels clearly until the cartridge has moved approximately 20 centimetres straight out to the side from the muzzles. This narrow vision around the focus is what I call "good vision". This has the shape of a narrow cone, with the tip in the pupil of the dominant eye. At the muzzles, the cone has a diameter of approximately 20 centimetres. Naturally, the diameter of the cone grows with distance. Test this by asking your partner to take one step backwards and hold the cartridge up again on the border of your good vision. The distance between the cartridge and the rib's extended centre line naturally becomes greater in centimetres calculated on the longer distance to the cartridge. On the other hand, the angle as such hasn't changed! At the muzzles, the distance straight out to the side is still approximately 20 centimetres, calculated from the rib's centre line.

Both of the inner visions - focus and good vision - are vital keys to successful game shooting. They are the most important fundamental components in the starting point that I cover in the next lesson.

Before we conclude, I would like to ask you to carry out another experiment. Ask your partner to step back about five metres. Then proceed as before. Focus on the cartridge while your partner moves it straight out to the side. When the cartridge reaches the border of good vision, you should change your focus and look at the barrels instead.

What happened?

You lost the target, didn't you? Now imagine that you are focusing on a bird approximately 25 metres away. If you lose sight of the bird and focus on the barrels, then it definitely is out of the picture. Accordingly, your fine motor control as directed by your eye is also disengaged. If you do this while you are swinging through for a moving target, the swing will stop and you almost inevitably will shoot behind.

Rule of thumb number eleven - Focus and "good vision" are the two most vital abilities for game shooting.

Naturally, there is an aesthetic aspect to game shooting...

... A male pheasant comes flying high over the tops of the trees, illuminated by a sinking evening sun. A straight incoming shot. Directly overhead. The pheasant's flight path ends abruptly. A few slowly descending feathers float in a ray of sun. Nature's circle of life is complete.

Pheasant a'la Coq au Vin

INGREDIENTS FOR 4 PORTIONS

2 x skinned pheasants, cut into 8 pieces
15 x small onions
2 x leeks in pieces
20 x field mushrooms
1 x turnip in pieces
2 x apples in pieces
2 x cloves of garlic
3 dl dry cider
2 dl dry white wine
Thyme
Finely chopped parsley
Salt and pepper
Oil
Maizena or arrowroot

COOKING PROCESS
Heat up the oil in a frying pan
Brown the pieces of pheasant, small onions,
leeks, garlic and turnip for 10 minutes
Add cider, thyme and white wine
Braise under a lid until the meat is soft

Thicken with Maizena or arrowroot
Add the pieces of apple and sprinkle over
the parsley
Serve with boiled rice

(The dish tastes best if it can absorb
all the flavourings until the next day)

LESSON TWELVE
THE STARTING POINT

I said earlier that you should mount behind the bird and swing through, focusing on the target.

The question you naturally ask is: "How far behind the target should I mount?" You have likely worked out that if you mount far behind the bird, then you have to swing quickly to catch up. Or if you mount close behind the target, you can swing very slowly and still catch up.

We established earlier that timing means time required, and that you should swing from the starting point behind the bird, up to and through it at the same speed irrespective of whether the bird is flying quickly or slowly. Swing time controls swing speed, which in turn controls the lead. This is thanks to the law of inertia and the time delay at the firing signal that we covered in Lesson Nine.

So the problem is: Where should you start so that the distance from the starting point up to the bird is always the same? If the distance is different each time, then the swing speed will also be different each time. If you have a different swing speed through a target that passes with exactly the same speed and at exactly the same distance each time, then the lead naturally will be different. This is because the time delay, from when the brain gives the command to shoot to when the shot is actually fired, is always the same.

What you need is a starting point that is the same every time you mount. The solution to this problem lies in the "good vision" that we covered in the previous lesson.

As you now know, good vision forms a cone with a diameter of approximately 40 centimetres at the muzzles when you fix your focus at a target over the barrels (20 centimetres on each side of the centre of the rib).

This is a fact of which you now will take advantage. When you detect the bird, focus on it and mount on the point where you first saw it (the barrels should follow behind the target with 20 centimetres air gap at the muzzle). The barrels are then pointing towards a point somewhere in the vicinity of the outer edge of the good vision cone. You have the perfect starting point at this point!

So how will this work? First and foremost, as you remember from Lesson Ten, we human beings, thanks to visual memory, can keep a large number of things in mind while we focus on an object (such as a football player's passing and "eye" for the game at the end of that lesson).

Now replace "eye" for the game with "eye" for the starting point and line of flight. Despite the fact that you are focused on the target the entire time, good vision and visual memory help you aim the barrels at exactly the right point behind the bird. You have no idea how far behind the bird the barrels are pointing in terms of metres, but you know that you mount equally as far behind the bird every time - IN TERMS OF THE ANGLE! You also know that the distance - that is the angle from the mounting point and up to the bird - is always the same irrespective of how far away, how quickly or how slowly it is flying.

The starting point is decisive for whether you hit or miss when shooting a moving target. Exactly how the starting point looks is an individual matter. On the other hand, it generally is true that when you have found your own individual starting point, you "sense" both the bird and the barrels without needing to aim.

As good vision is shaped like a narrow cone (a fact which I repeat), you realise that the distance of the starting point of the barrels behind the bird grows with the distance between you and the bird. However, and here's the beauty of it, the angle between the starting point and the bird is always the same irrespective of how far away the bird is.

Time for another small digression. What is "fast" and what

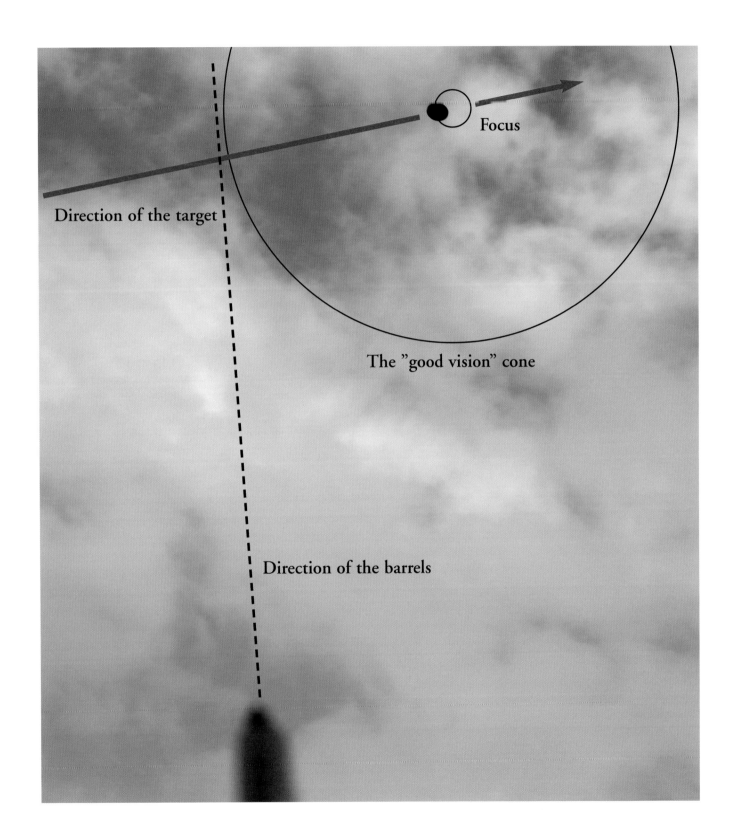

Focus

Direction of the target

The "good vision" cone

Direction of the barrels

is "slow"? How fast does a jumbo jet fly? You perceive it to fly very slowly due to the long distance you view it from. How quickly does a mouse run? You perceive it to run very fast due to the short distance between you and the mouse.

Now think of your swing as a circle, and you are standing in the centre of the circle. All you need to do is to move the barrels from the starting point and past the bird. If the bird is flying quickly (that is, passing close to you), your eye registers this and your fine motor control reacts to the information. Your built-in clock - in other words, your timing - advises you when you must swing quickly. When the barrels pass the bird, the swing speed accordingly is high. If the bird is flying slowly (that is, passing further from you), your eye registers this and your fine motor control corrects itself according to the information. Your built-in clock advises you that there is no hurry here. You swing smoothly and calmly. In both cases, with either a fast or slow target, the lead will be exactly correct thanks to the "law of inertia." (Study the illustrations in Lesson Nine carefully and the connection will become clear).

One further observation after you have found your starting point. In the previous lesson, I asserted that when the starting point is correct, you can "sense" both the bird and the barrels. I can also say that if you mount too closely behind the bird, your body will "sense" it when you swing. You sense that you have no power, that is to say, speed in the swing! Accordingly, you have no "automatic" lead either.

I will refer again to the above paragraph when we review common mistakes when shooting departing quarry under natural conditions. Many students become stressed and believe that they won't be able to manage shooting before the target is out of range. During mounting, they forget the starting point and mount almost on the centre of the bird. The swing has no speed, the lead is too small and the charge of shot passes behind the target.

I have dedicated many words to the starting point, and I have done so for a reason - You must always have the same starting point for all shooting angles! Accordingly, the starting point is exactly the same whether you are shooting incoming, crossing or going away targets.

It is difficult to practise the starting point in a living room. Clearly, you can fix on a point on the ceiling moulding that is located so that the corner of the room is precisely at the outer limit of the good vision cone. You can then practise focusing on the selected point and mount so that the barrels are pointing exactly towards the corner.

If you do this, then we can wrap up this part so far. You now know from the lesson on the stock that you can mount on a point you are looking at without "aiming." If the mount is correct, then the barrels are directed to the point without you needing to check. The idea of the dry run in the earlier section (Lesson Five) was that you should be firmly convinced that this actually is the case. The idea of the dry run in this section has exactly the same objective. The difference here is that you are focusing on a point somewhere on the ceiling moulding while you are mounting on the corner. The good vision and visual memory are your reliable allies. Despite you focusing somewhere else on the ceiling moulding, the barrels actually are pointing towards the corner. Practise these dry runs until you are firmly convinced that this really is also the case here!

Naturally, practising dry runs is always good and reinforces self-confidence, but it is only on the shooting field that everything is for "real" so to speak. There you will immediately learn whether your starting point is right or wrong. I cannot maintain enough here that a good shooting instructor is really beneficial for getting things right from the very start. Accordingly, a few shooting lessons are truly a good investment.

In the coming lessons - the practical section - I will use the term "starting point" quite often. Repeat the previous lesson and review it very carefully. It will be easier if you really concentrate on all the factors affecting the starting point.

So now to rule of thumb number twelve - The right starting point means a hit. The wrong starting point means a miss!

Ryan is something of a philosopher.

... A sceptic in the spirit of Francis Bacon. He doesn't say much, but listens more. Often contributing with the decisive comment. He told me once that he had taken a tour of a coastal church. While seeing the sights, he was taken to a painting with many names. The guide said that a ship had gone down outside the reef in a storm, and that the painting had all the names of those who had prayed to Our Lord and were rescued. Ryan thought for a moment and then asked where the other painting was hung. "Which painting?" asked the guide. "The one with the names of all those who prayed to Our Lord and were not saved," commented Ryan.

Such is Ryan. He doesn't say much and hates giving speeches. We were guests one time at a family shoot. A white pheasant came flying at Ryan at a perfect height, a perfect angle and with a perfect speed. Ryan lifted the shotgun in the ready position and waited. And waited. And waited. Finally, his shooting neighbour couldn't wait any longer and shot. The white pheasant fell. Ryan turned to him smiling and bowed. "Why didn't you shoot?" I asked. "The poor devil doesn't know that the person shooting the white pheasant has to give the dinner speech," said Ryan. Luckily, Ryan's gun was a brilliant speaker. But that is another story.

LESSON THIRTEEN
ALWAYS MOUNT ON THE BIRD WITH YOUR FRONT HAND LEADING YOUR BODY

We reviewed in Lesson Two why the shotgun looks the way it does. In Lesson Five, we came to the conclusion that the mount should always be with the shotgun at a 45-degree angle to the upper body. When you mount, you should only need to move the shotgun forwards and upwards, led by the front hand.

Now there are exceptions where you detect a bird at an angle of exactly 45-degrees. What do you do?

If the bird is flying on a lower trajectory, you need only move your weight onto your front foot at the same time as you lean slightly forwards. If it is flying higher, you need only move your weight onto your rear foot and lean slightly backwards. It is as simple as that.

One fundamental mistake that many guns make under stress is that they remain in the ready position, "jerk" the stock up to their shoulder and then aim the barrels to the mounting point. The mount (see Lesson Four) and the starting point are then wrong, which in turn negatively affects the entire swing process. What you should consider, and this is something you can practise at home in the living room, is always moving your body towards the target led by your front hand. This applies to all shooting angles - incoming as much as crossing and going away targets.

Rule of thumb number thirteen - It is always the forend hand - the front hand - that leads during mounting.

Experienced bird dog handlers claim...

... that there are two types of pointing dogs - searchers and finders. The first are characterized by long searches, boring straight out into the wind and not much more. The latter are characterized by an irregular search pattern and constant deviations to end up in the right place in spite of the poor scent a stressed bird emanates. The searchers' graceful run back and forth is a joy to see. The finders' work efforts often result in a heavy burden to carry.

LESSON FOURTEEN
THE ACCELERATING SWING

It's finally time to examine the swing as such.

By an accelerating swing, I mean a swing that starts out at the starting point and then smoothly accelerates up to and past the target. The speed of the acceleration is determined by your timing. Timing, in turn, is subordinate to the eye and focus, which perceive the speed of the target and automatically control the acceleration of the swing. As we established in the earlier lessons, you learned how to control this complicated process during childhood, although in other contexts, such as football, tennis, games, bicycling, etc. So the accelerating swing is already stored in your muscle memory.

Swinging is a natural movement. However... and this is something I'll demonstrate... in game shooting you can swing in two ways - with your body or with your arms.

Now let us agree on one thing, once and for all. If you swing with your arms, then it is less likely you will hit the target! In other words - you must always swing with your body!

Now imagine that your body is a kind of gun carriage, where the shotgun is securely bolted into your shoulder, pointing at a 45-degree angle to the sky. You cannot move the shotgun in any way other than by turning. If you want to raise the barrels, you must lean backwards. If you want to lower them, you must lean forwards. If you want to turn them straight to the side, you must turn the entirety of your upper body. If you want to turn them diagonally upwards, you must angle your upper body by sliding one hip straight out to the side. The centre for all movement is located in the waist and hips. A certain amount of footwork needs to be added to this. For example, a golfer will transfer his weight to his back foot when moving the club backwards. When he then swings forward, he transfers his weight to his front foot. The same footwork applies for shooting as for tennis, table tennis and other ball sports.

I would like to make another observation here, one that you will discover when it's time to shoot "for real". A good swing always starts from the feet. If you are standing correctly, as I demonstrated in Lesson One, the swing will be right.

Now stand up straight and comfortably, and turn your upper body to the left and then to the right. You will notice that your footwork and the weight transfer from foot to foot take care of themselves. You will also discover that it is easier to turn to the side if you lift the heel of the foot on which your bodyweight is not resting.

THIS IS SOMETHING YOU ALREADY KNOW – AND NOW YOU KNOW IT EVEN BETTER!

Clasp your hands and point straightforward with straight arms. Point to the centre of the living room wall. Then "swing" to one corner and then back. Continue to swing to the other corner. If you are standing "correctly," you will have no problem with your footwork. The weight transfer from one foot to the other takes place naturally.

How wide an arc can you swing through? This naturally depends on how old and supple you are. Test how large a circle sector you can swing through with your arms straightforward and your hands clasped. I am sure that you can manage 180-degrees from side to side without any effort.

Now you should try another swing - shooting an incoming target straight overhead. You can easily lean backwards (with your weight on your back foot) so that you are pointing straight up to the ceiling. I would argue that you could point even further back if it was really necessary.

When shooting at a moving target according to the "Natural Way", you are simply doing what your body already is capable of. You also know from Lesson Eight that motion memory is in the large muscles. I will now prove that this is the case, because you will now make a swing that many have difficulty with before they learn how it's done. You will also

have a shotgun in your hands this time.

What you will do now is a diagonal swing. Stand several metres from the living room wall and mount on the corner down at the floor. If you are a right-handed gun, then it's easiest to mount on the corner to the right. If left-handed, then it's easiest to mount on the corner to the left. From there, you will swing at an angle of 45-degrees up to the ceiling. Do this several times and then think about why it feels so awkward.

Put your shotgun down and make the same movement with arms straight and hands clasped in the same manner as before. Now it's easy as pie, isn't it? But why? You probably leaned to the side by sliding your hip out so that your upper body tilted. At the same time, you lowered one of your shoulders. When you do this, your shoulder area is parallel with the diagonal line. When you "swing" diagonally in this way, you turn your upper body in exactly the same way as when you "swing" horizontally from corner to corner. Now try to do this in the same way with the shotgun in your hands. As you notice, you want to angle the shotgun slightly so that it is in contact with your shoulder and cheek in the same way as when you stand upright and swing. Perfect! If you check, you will see that the barrels and rib are parallel with the imagined

line of flight. I bet the diagonal swing now feels considerably less awkward.

The question is why does it feel so awkward to make a diagonal swing without tilting your upper body and lowering one shoulder. Quite simply, this is because you have to raise the shotgun with your arms so that the muzzles follow the line of flight, and swing the shotgun with your arms instead of with your body, something we established was wrong at the beginning of this lesson.

Now look at the illustrations. What they show are the fundamentals in the different swings - the straight side, the straight incoming and the diagonal swings. While you are looking at the illustrations, you should also reflect over how small the movements required for a long swing are. This is because while making these movements, I am standing in the centre of the circle and turning my upper body around its own axis.

This last observation is good to keep in mind each time you are standing on a peg or out in the shooting field. You

have plenty of time to make these small movements. Lifting the shotgun from the ready position up to your cheek is something that is done in fractions of a second. Rotating your upper body from the starting point and accelerating the swing through the target also takes just a brief moment. I'll reveal a small secret of the trade here. The students who I have mount and shoot in slow motion, shoot the bird earlier than they do when they are in a hurry, because they believe that they are pressed for time. If you work in the right way with your body, then there is no such thing as being pressed for time - you have as much time as you want!

Rule of thumb number fourteen - Take it easy. There is no such thing as being pressed for time. One RIGHT movement is faster than two quick movements! HURRY SLOWLY! A calm correct movement is faster than two or three quick movements that have to be corrected.

At the end of the 1800s...

...seventy percent of the Swedish population worked on farms or in the forests. The homes were small and hunting contributed significantly to the household. An acquaintance of mine, now old and grey, financed his first confirmation suit by selling squirrel skins to furriers in Tranås. One learned young to live with and in nature. Knowledge about hunting and fishing was inherited from father to son. It was a big day when a ten-year old was seen to be ready to shoot his first hare or pigeon. Today, the farms are large and the farmers few. Children who have had the privilege of growing up in close contact with nature move to the suburbs. Old hunting traditions are going to their graves. Or are they? The growing interest in shooting and experiences in the wild attract more and more people. Hopefully, our ancient traditions will enjoy a renaissance.

LESSON FIFTEEN
SHOOTING GOING AWAY BIRDS

Now we will do what I call a "Skalman," which I have named after a Swedish cartoon character, a tortoise who sticks his head far out of his shell forwards and upwards. Pretend you are shooting over a bird dog on point. The principle, of course, is that the dog points to the bird in front of it by freezing into a statue. It stands. You follow up behind the dog and urge it forwards. If everything works as it should, the bird takes flight.

You realise the importance of really holding the barrels parallel to the ground so that mounting and shooting always take place above the dog in front of you. So why not be safe instead of sorry and aim the barrels high up into the air? You already know the answer. If you hold the barrels up, it is easy for the barrels to sink down - more towards the dog instead of up from the dog. I usually say to my students that a straight shot at a going away target is like trying to stab the bird with a bayonet fixed to the barrels. It is important that the body, head and shotgun follow the bayonet forwards.

Very many guns find shooting departing targets difficult. This is because the shot requires real movement forwards. First of all, you have to transfer your weight to your front foot and really lean your upper body forward in order to be able to mount correctly. It's still a question of the barrels being at a 45-degree angle to your upper body. In order for the shotgun to reach your cheek in the right way, you must also really move your head forward, at the same time as lifting it slightly. Try this mount and then straighten your back. You will discover that you have exactly the same mount as when you mount for flying shots at a 45-degree upwards angle. You can even see that you should always have the same mount irrespective of whether you are shooting incoming, crossing or going away targets or shooting against ground targets!

Otherwise, you shoot in the same way as before. You mount on the point where you detected the bird - the correct starting point - and swing through with the correct speed in relation to the movement of the target. That is, the right

"timing." You never defocus from the target. You swing as before, from the starting point and past the bird. As you pass the bird, you pull the trigger in the centre of the target.

Many shots have a tendency to become stressed when shooting going away targets. They believe that the bird will fly out of range before they manage to fire a shot. The bird, of course, is already tens of metres away when the gun sees it, but when making such a shot, you are working with very, very small movements. In a "Skalman" position, lifting the shotgun correctly up to your cheek, you have it in position within a fraction of a second. The movement and change in angle in order to catch up to the bird is unimaginably small. In either case, it doesn't matter if the bird is flying straight away from you or out at an angle. I promise that you have plenty of time. In addition, I dare promise that you will hit the bird if you pull the trigger when the barrels pass the target and you really continue the swing through. The trick is never losing focus on the target or trying to aim!

With straight shots at targets going away, it seems that the brain is extra anxious to take command. It is tempting to aim to try to get better accuracy, and it is always as disastrous!

A common mistake when shooting going away targets is forgetting that the upper body controls the swing. It is easy to allow your arms to take over here and swing the shotgun. If you miss such a shot, you should ask yourself six things:

1. Was the mount correct?
2. Was I in a hurry?
3. Did I have the right starting point?
4. Did I aim?
5. Did I swing with both arms or with my upper body?
6. Did I shoot decisively?

There are major similarities when shooting going away targets and against ground targets. It you are shooting a hare on the run, your mount is the same as discussed above. Firmly with your weight on your front foot, lean and move your shoulder forward so that the heel rests firmly against your shoulder on mounting. You have the same starting point here as when shooting flying targets and you swing in the same way. The difference really is a matter of detail. It is easy for your eyes to "fix" on the ground. In order to avoid this, I shut one eye. This is a personal idiosyncrasy. The fundamental rule is that all shots must be shot in accordance with the same basic principle. This applies in 90 - 95 % of all shooting angles. In other cases, every individual gun must adopt their "own" trick for individual shots. Personally, I shut one eye, just to avoid fixing my stare at the ground. This way I force myself to swing through ground targets in the right way.

Rule of thumb number fifteen - Transfer your weight firmly to your front foot with your knee bent, move forwards with your upper body, push your neck forward and really lift your head when mounting on low targets!

According to old traditions...

...the hunters from the village gather to shoot the all White Mountain hares. The hares will then hang from the windows on the south sides of the houses, stuffed with juniper and twigs for tenderising and taste. Still, beautiful December mornings with new snow, a couple of degrees below zero, are one of the high points of the shooting season. Harriers bark. An entrance hole. Is that where the hare has its burrow?

LESSON SIXTEEN
SECOND BARREL KILLS AND SHOOTING PAIRS

Second barrel kills and shooting pairs of targets, doublé, are two totally separate disciplines. However, I have chosen to treat them in one lesson here in order to explain the difference.

Second barrel kills are when the first shot misses and a gun makes a new attempt to hit the target. If the mount, starting point and swing were correct from the beginning, the barrels followed the target's flight path and passed through it. A miss can be due to many things. The absolutely most common reason for a miss is that the gun switches focus from the target to the barrels and then aims. The swing then stops, the charge of shot passes behind the bird and possibly a little low.

Of course, everything is ready for a second shot. All you really need to do is focus on the target, let it pass, find your starting point, swing to catch up again, pull the trigger and complete the swing without stopping. This time, with your focus on the target - not on the barrels. The second shot now has a good chance of a good hit. This often takes place completely automatically as the gun doesn't have time for "precision shooting" but instead allows the body to take care of the movement and feeling. The latter is a synthesis of how the "Natural Way" works in practice!

Shooting pairs of targets, doublé, in contrast with second barrel kills, consists of two totally separate mountings.

First, you shoot the bird exactly as you have been taught. You assume the ready position, mount behind the bird (starting point), swing to catch up and through, pull the trigger when you pass the target and carry on swinging.

NOW TO THE SECOND TARGET.
WHAT DO YOU DO?

Lower the stock from your shoulder and cheek. Turn your body towards the new target. Mount again. Find the new starting point. Swing to catch up. Pull the trigger when the barrels pass the bird and carry on swinging.

YOU HAVE MOUNTED TWICE
AND SHOT TWO BIRDS.

I have claimed several times that you gain time when you do a perfect mount based on a correct starting position. It then is a question of small movements without the need for time-consuming corrections to end up "right."

What happens if you allow the shotgun to remain on your shoulder and move directly to the second bird when you are shooting a pair? A shotgun weighs around 3.5 kilograms and the resistance generated is considerable. You probably would be in the wrong position right from the start and it's not certain that you would be able to correct it. This means that you start the swing from a point that is not in the bird's line of

132

flight. As a consequence, you swing diagonally through the target. You shoot over or under depending on how the target is flying. With almost one hundred percent certainty, you will also shoot behind.

You can practise dry runs of both second barrel kills and shooting pairs at home in your living room by following the ceiling mouldings.

You can practise second barrel kills by identifying two points at a suitable distance from each other on the same moulding. You pull the trigger only when you pass the first, stop and then continue the swing towards and through the second.

You can practise shooting pairs against two ceiling mouldings that meet in a corner. Pick out a point on each ceiling moulding. Mount on the corner and swing through the first point. Pull the trigger as the chosen point. Lower the shotgun from your cheek and shoulder. Turn towards the corner again. Mount, swing along the second ceiling moulding and pull the trigger. If you find this exercise monotonous, you can swing in the other direction, that is mount on a point roughly in the middle of the moulding and swing in towards the corner.

Rule of thumb number sixteen - Shooting a pair of birds always involves two shots that are completely separate from each other!
IMPORTANT: Shooting a pair cannot come into question until the first target has been hit. Etiquette dictates that the first bird always has the right to two shots if necessary to complete the kill. If the first shot makes a hit, then you have a "bonus" shot if there is a further target to shoot. There are no pairs in the plural, only one single target for each shot.

Halland has never...

...produced any skiers as far as I know. The flat fields located near the sea are often bare and free of snow the entire winter, but every now and then, a front of wet snow marches over the landscape. The alert ears of brown hares then suddenly become visible against the white background. One needs only to crouch down to find them. The trick of getting within shooting distance is learned quickly. One can never go directly towards the quarry. A path twenty metres out to the side makes the hare uncertain. Should it stay low or flee? With the shotgun ready and a measured approach, the hare's hesitation could be fatal.

LESSON SEVENTEEN
STATIONARY TARGETS AND JUDGING DISTANCE

Shooting a sitting hare (or bird) is a completely different discipline compared to shooting a moving target. Here you need to be accurate and aim!

When shooting moving targets, focus and fine motor control direct the shotgun. When shooting a stationary target, it is the brain and sight picture that take over.

Mounting, in contrast, is the same as for shooting moving targets. You transfer your weight to your front foot. Lean your body forward so that the shotgun is at a 45-degree angle against your shoulder. Move your head forward (do a "Skalman"). Mount. What then remains is to align the shotgun to the target so that the sight picture corresponds with the image you learned earlier by practice-shooting against set up clay pigeons, for example.

It is also important to practise shooting stationary targets, despite such shooting appearing to be reasonably easy. You can practise this type of shooting by setting up clay pigeons against a steep grassy bank or other safe background and then pacing out at a shooting distance of around 25 metres. From there, you find the correct sight picture when the pigeons are hit and memorise it. Note that the standing clay pigeons are not blown into powder in the same way as they are when flying. This is because they are not rotating. Repeat this exercise at regular intervals so that the sight picture really does correspond as is necessary during a real shoot.

JUDGING DISTANCE

Learning to judge distance is a training process that you can practice every time you take a walk with or without a dog. Quite simply, you stop and try to judge the distance to a tree or object along the route. Then you pace out the distance to find out how accurate your judgement was.

The more often you practise judging distance, the more

certain you will become.

In order to be able to pace out a distance with a good degree of certainty, you can measure out 10 metres, for example, and then see how many double steps it takes to pace out the distance. Do the steps counting a number of times and at a normal walking pace, without striding them out. An individual of average height will move about 110 cm with a double step. Ten double steps are then approximately eleven metres.

Another way to judge distance is the "multiplying" method. If you are of an average height, around 180 centimetres, then imagine lying fully stretched on your stomach. Starting from these 180 centimetres, it is easy to "multiply" the length. Imagine that you are outstretched three times in a row so that the distance is just over 5 metres. Starting from that distance, you can then continue to "multiply" two, three, four or five times. You can judge short distances with very good accuracy using this method.

A third method for measuring distance when you are standing on a shooting peg in rugged terrain, for example, is to throw a stone that weighs roughly the same as a full cartridge (approximately 35 grams). If you don't throw with all your strength, and if you don't have javelin or shot put as a hobby, you'll throw the stone approximately 20 to 30 metres.

Good distance judgement is a must during shooting. As a shot, it is important that you determine your maximum shooting distance as soon as you stand on the shooting peg. A deer can be shot if it moves in front of a certain bush, for example. If the deer moves past it to the other side, the distance then is too great for a shot. A bird can be shot if it flies between or in front of two certain trees.

An average good shot has a good hit percentage at distances from around 20 to 25 metres. A really good game shot has good hits at distances from around 30 to 35 metres. That's where the limit is.

One facet of game shooting is that small errors are magnified with distance. For this reason, it is important to set your own limits - as well as more importantly, for ethical reasons. A person shooting outside of his or her own distance capacity almost inevitably only maims and causes unnecessary suffering to the game. Nor is it popular as a shooting guest to be too "trigger happy." Guns who fire at pheasants, ducks or pigeons at distances of up to 50 metres are looked upon with disapproval by shoot captains and rarely can count on new invitations. Naturally, the same rules apply when shooting ground game.

Rule of thumb number seventeen - Never overestimate your own shooting skills. While shooting - determine your distance limits as soon as you arrive at the shooting peg and stick to them rigidly!

One never ceases

...to be amazed by the behaviour of wild fowl when mating and hatching. Birds that normally are both vigilant and shy, don't move. They burrow deep down and are difficult to see. If you take a walk along the beach, you have to be careful not to walk on them. If you come too close to a nesting Eider, they can attack. Such behavioural changes and the desire to pass the gene pool on to new generations are fairly incomprehensible. The instinct to flee and the desire to survive become subordinate to a greater purpose. This dedication, or defiance of death if you wish to view it like that, is true for all species. Coming too close to a hatching kite can also be a hazardous business. The male approaches several centimetres overhead like a shot out of a cannon. It is impossible to not duck. It is wise then to keep both body and head out of the way. To be hit in the middle of your face by a bird weighing one kilo at that speed would probably even put Mohammed Ali down for the count.

The eggs and markings in the olden days were shrouded in mystery. Seers throughout the ages have used eggs to predict the future. The author, PC Jersild, writes in his novel, "The Return of the Geniuses," about the shaman egg readers who when winter came, wandered with their egg baskets and compared the markings with the surface of the moon. Based on the pattern of the egg, which can be as individual as a fingerprint, they could see who among the country folk had to be sacrificed to the god for the sun to return and new life to begin. Fiction, of course, but entirely plausible. Not even in our enlightened time can one avoid being surprised over the miracles nature provides when giving birth to birds for millions of years and guaranteeing the survival of the species.

LESSON EIGHTEEN
AND NOW, OUT INTO THE REAL WORLD

If you have worked through, thought about and practised the exercises that I have suggested, I guess you are now keen to try clay pigeon shooting for real.

If you have access to your own clay target trap, you can just start.

If you've thought about getting your own clay target trap, I would then like to recommend that you purchase a strong and stable model. The spring should be powerful enough to throw a clay pigeon 70 to 80 metres and preferably longer.

If you don't have access to a suitable piece of ground for private clay pigeon shooting, you need to contact a shooting field. There are a number of good grounds to choose from. Sporting ranges are perhaps the most suitable. In general, you then have the opportunity to practise the five basic shots - incoming, crossing shots from the right, crossing shots from the left, going away and targets simulating ground game.

Naturally, skeet and trap shooting ranges are also suitable, but with one reservation. The springs on the traps are often set so that the pigeons fly a little fast to begin with. In many cases, if you talk to whoever is responsible for the facility, you can ask whether the speed can be reduced slightly. If you can borrow or hire a range when it's not in use, you can rehearse shots from different angles without feeling pressured by an audience.

The alternative, and now I'm not just talking about myself, is to start shooting with a shooting instructor. You not only get the basics then, but also advice on how to arrange your own practices in the future.

Of course, rabbits are soft...

...and cute, but if they get a chance to reproduce in the wild, they quickly become a plague. To stand over a rabbit hole and let a ferret in is a strange experience. One suddenly can feel the vibrations underfoot and the rabbits come out running. Events happen quickly. The opportunity to shoot is over in a minute or two. A little later, a totally white ferret comes out. If not, he probably has killed under ground, eaten the rabbit and gone to sleep. Then you can expect a long wait.

LESSON NINETEEN
SHOOTING INCOMING TARGETS

Straight incoming shots are considered by many to be the simplest shots. The shot consists of mounting plus a swing. A straight incoming shot therefore should not present any major problems. This is what the process looks like step by step:

- Adopt the ready position as we have gone through.
- Hold the shotgun at a 45-degree angle in relation to your upper body as early as the ready position.
- When the bird comes, focus on it and don't defocus even for a moment.
- Mount "actively" behind the bird by transferring your body weight to your front foot while you move the shotgun forwards and upwards with your front hand.
  The hand gripping the small of the stock needs only follow.
- The stock comes up to your cheek.
- Starting behind the target, you are in line with the target's flight path.
- Accelerate the swing calmly, while you transfer your body weight to your rear foot.
- Swing through the target.
- Pull the trigger when the bird disappears behind the barrels.
- Then the subsequent delay, which gives the "right" lead.
- The shot is fired.
- Continue the follow through with the swing through.

These twelve steps summed up are: Mount behind, accelerate the swing, swing through and pull the trigger.

A common mistake when shooting incoming birds is that you only lift up the shotgun and mount in front of the target, which is coming at a high speed. The barrels stop and you don't get any speed in the swing. You miss behind. (See steps 2, 4 and 5 above.)

Another common mistake is that you keep your body weight on your front foot during the swing. (See steps 4 and 5 above.) If you keep your body weight on your front foot, you have to move your lower body far forward and really lean backwards without actually going particularly far back. The result is that there is resistance and the swing is slowed with the consequence being a poor hit or miss.

Another effect of allowing your body weight to remain on your front foot is that it could lead to you lifting your head in order to be able to follow the target with your eye. Your cheek loses contact with the stock. This changes the relationship between eye, rib and muzzles. The barrels no longer point in the direction you are looking. Right-handed guns will shoot to the left of the target. Left-handed guns will shoot to the right of the target. In both cases, it results in a poor shot or miss.

Another common mistake is you don't hold the barrels up properly in the ready position. (See step 2 above.) When the bird comes, you lift the stock up to your shoulder with your front hand. (Right mount, see steps 4 and 5 above.) You have two problems then at the small of the stock. One - the barrels rotate around your front hand, right across the target's flight path. The shotgun movement is too expansive and you don't have any real control of the shotgun. Two - the stock can end up far out on your shoulder and you have to tilt your head to get cheek contact. This results in a low mount, poor hit or miss - and it hurts!

If you do hit the target - don't be in a hurry to shoot a new bird. Instead, run the entire process over in your head. Try to remember how the starting point looked, how the swing and weight transfer from front to rear foot progressed, as well as the moment of firing and the swing through.

If you miss - run the shot through in your mind and ask: "Did I meet the bird with my body by moving the shotgun

forwards and upwards under guidance of the front hand? Did I have the correct starting point and did I focus at the starting point? Did I defocus from the target and check the direction of the barrels, in other words, did I aim during the swing? Did I check the direction of the barrels (aimed) just before they passed by the bird?" You probably will come to one of the following three answers. One - you were careless or in too much of a hurry during mounting. Two - you weren't focused on the bird the entire time. Three - you thought that you were focusing on the bird when actually you were looking at it with your "wide vision."

If you were in too much of a hurry, the remedy is simple. Hurry slowly! Act extra calmly during mounting when you shoot the next bird. You have plenty of time. You will even discover that you shoot the bird faster!

Did you lose focus on the bird or look with your "wide vision" - if so, then concentrate and focus firmly on the front edge of the bird during the next attempt.

Finally - practise dry runs with mounting, transferring your body weight and swing in accordance with the above steps. The more you are at one with the gun, the more certain you will be. Practising dry runs at home in the living room gives direct results on the shooting field. As well as on the shooting peg!

Good luck!

Summary - Start behind, accelerate through the target and pull the trigger.

Maps and compasses...

...are indispensable aids at shoots in large forests. An acquaintance who has always relied on his sense of direction and memory for locations, suddenly disappeared one day. Towards evening he called me on his mobile telephone and said that he was lost and standing on a gravel road by the remains of an old cottage.

Despite our maps, we could not help him find the way. Then one of our shooting companions suddenly got an idea. He called the local taxi-driver and described the surroundings to him. It worked. The taxi trip ended up being 34 kilometres.

LESSON TWENTY
PURE CROSSING SHOTS (FOREHAND)

For a right-handed gun, the forehand swing is for birds flying to the left. The bird comes from the right and flies to the left. For a left-handed gun, it is the reverse - the bird flies to the right. The bird comes from the left and flies to the right.

The position of your feet is the same as when shooting incoming quarry, but the difference is that your body weight should now rest on your front foot, and you should turn your upper body from your hips. In order to facilitate the turn, you lift the heel of either your right foot (if a right-handed gun) or your left foot (if left-handed). Now you can easily cover a semicircle. This is more than sufficient.

Precisely as with shooting incoming birds, it is important that the entire process - from the ready position to the swing through - takes place calmly and methodically. Mount behind the target. Make sure that the stock slides up to your cheek without tilting your head so that your cheek has the correct contact with the stock. Find your starting point. Focus on the target. Swing to catch up and pass. Pull the trigger when the muzzles pass the bird. This is where the delay will automatically result in the correct lead. The actual shot will follow and finally swing through without slowing down. All in one single synchronised movement. Simple? Actually not really. The desire to hit the target is greater than the desire to do things right.

However, there is one difficulty that you should always bear in mind. It concerns finding and following the bird's line of flight. I covered this very carefully in the previous lesson, but I'll cover it again! You find the line of flight by tilting the shotgun so that the rib follows parallel along it. The turning takes place in your shoulders. Quite simply, you raise the shoulder that is turned in line with the bird flight at the same time as you angle your hip. A right-handed gun raises the left shoulder (left shot) and a left-handed gun raises the right (right shot). Now you can follow the line of flight by turning your upper body. You don't need any help from your arms.

When shooting, you rarely stand waiting in the starting position on the shooting peg. An exercise that you can, and

should, include when you practise is to start from the position and posture you normally have on the shooting peg. When the bird comes - first move the shotgun to the starting position. Don't be in a hurry, you have plenty of time. Then mount and shoot as above. The reason you have plenty of time is that the swing itself is a relatively small angled movement. Even if the target is flying fast and the shot is a long one, the rotation in the centre - where you are standing - is quite small. The most important aspect here is a good mount.

A SUMMARY FOR WHEN
YOU SHOOT CROSSING SHOTS:

- Check that you have the right starting position.
- Be exact with the position of your feet (absolutely do not stand with your legs apart).
- Transfer your body weight to your front foot. Left foot for right-handed guns and right foot for left-handed guns.
- Focus on the target.
- Turn your shoulders and the shotgun so that the rib is parallel with the target's line of flight.
- Mount on the point where you first saw the bird, find your starting point and move the shotgun calmly forwards and upwards with your front hand so that the stock slides into the correct position against your shoulder, and turn your head (without tilting) so that the comb is in contact with your cheek at the height of the upper row of your teeth.
- Swing through the target and reduce the restriction of your body by lifting your rear heel.
- Pull the trigger when the barrels pass the target.
- The subsequent delay will result in the correct lead.
- The shot is fired.
- Continue with the swing through.

Summary - Start behind, swing through and pull the trigger when the barrels pass the target.

The old folks still speak...

... longingly of shoots for wood and black grouse. In those days, you found your hide while it was still dark. The equipment was simple. A Belgian made shotgun, significantly tight choked and wolf shot in the cartridge. While the cock grouse was enraptured, you wriggled forward to be within range. Metre by metre. A successful day could produce a half dozen cock grouse for dinner. The old folks said it was good for the lineage, shooting the old sterile cock grouse giving the young and healthy finally their chance with the hens. This isn't the case today. Such shoots are associated with a dim and distant past. Nowadays, it's about hunting with dogs that bark under the tree where the bird is hiding. But the advance is just as demanding. Game birds are timid and ready to take flight. Nine times out of ten, it is a ball shot at long distance on a sitting bird. Occasionally there is the chance to down a cock grouse in flight using a shotgun. It is a powerful experience.

LESSON TWENTY-ONE
PURE CROSSING SHOTS (BACKHAND)

For a right-handed gun, the backhand swing is for birds flying to the right. The bird comes from the left and flies to the right. For a left-handed gun, it is the reverse - birds coming from the right and flying to the left.

This is where the position of your feet is the be-all and end-all. The backhand swing requires that you really can rotate your body from your hips. For this reason, it is particularly important that you move your entire body weight to your rear foot - to the outside of the foot, so that you almost strain it. It is easy to lock your front leg during the swing itself. A tip: relax your front heel so that only your toes are in contact with the ground. In addition, allow your front knee to follow in the direction of the swing and don't bend your rear leg where your entire weight should be resting.

The backhand swing is difficult and a common mistake is that your body doesn't manage to rotate properly. The swing stops. The result - you are late and shoot behind. A subsequent mistake, when your body doesn't manage to maintain the swing, is that you roll your upper body instead of rotating it. The result - you shoot both under and behind.

Another common mistake is that when your body doesn't manage to rotate further, your arms take over and move the shotgun in a lateral sideways movement. When you move the shotgun in this way, you no longer are swinging. The result - a miss.

As the backhand swing feels difficult, my advice is that you practise dry runs as often as you can. Pay attention to the rolling of the upper body and parallel movement with your arms. When you have found the right footwork, the backhand swing will be considerably easier.

The mount and swing are always the same irrespective of which angles you shoot. Exactly as with all other shots, it is important that the entire process - from the ready position to the swing through- takes place calmly and methodically. Mount behind the target. Make sure that the stock slides up to your cheek. Focus continuously on the target. Find your starting point. Swing to catch up and through. Pull the trigger when the muzzles pass the bird. The delay will automatically result in the correct lead. The shot is fired. Continue with the swing through.

Summary - Start behind, swing through and pull the trigger when the barrels pass the target.

Those who claim that dogs lack the ability...

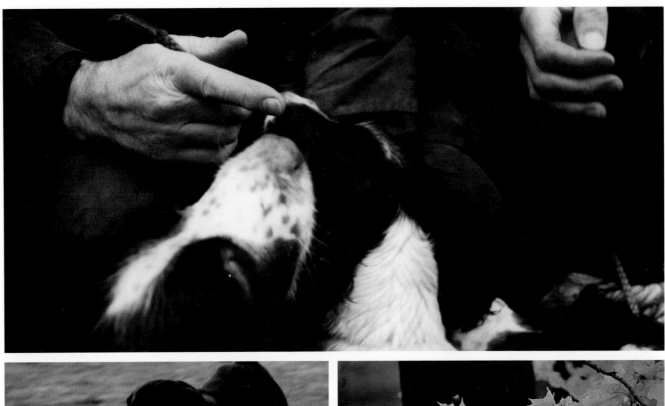

... to think logically have never met Benny. Benny is a sour old Springer. From his earliest days with Bill Denham, Benny occupied the most comfortable chair in the gunroom. I didn't know that then, but would soon be told. During a pigeon shoot, Benny carefully and meticulously executed his retrieving. A skilled retriever without doubt. After the shoot and dinner, Benny had not yet assumed his place. Alone in the room, and not knowing Benny's idiosyncrasies, I commanded "Down." Benny lifted an eyebrow and probably wondered if I had taken leave of my senses. After three repeats, and with the assistance of the most threatening body language I could summon, Benny reluctantly

moved and went out into the hall. When Bill's wife Sue came in with the whiskey tray, she almost dropped it from sheer surprise. No one had ever previously succeeded in driving Benny away from his favourite place. It was a pleasant evening followed by a good night's sleep. The next morning, my boots were gone. I found them eventually. Chewed up in the gunroom. Benny lay snoring in the most comfortable chair as always. Bill, who had helped me look, came in a moment later. He saw the devastation. "An example of a well thought out revenge" was his only comment. Benny didn't bat en eyelid.

SLIGHTLY ANGLED, HIGH CROSSING SHOTS (A SPECIAL VARIANT)

This is a special exercise with a special objective. This is where you discover the importance of leaning your upper body so that your shoulder section is parallel with the target's line of flight. This way, your swing follows the line of flight without you needing to use your arms for help.

To practise these shoots, proceed as follows. Position yourself so that you have a straight incoming target.

If you are a right-handed gun, you now walk several metres to the right at a right angle in relation to the bird's line of flight. You will then shoot towards the bird passing high up and to your left. If you are left-handed, you do the same thing, except in reverse. You walk several metres to the left and shoot towards the bird passing high up and to your right. This is the easiest side swing (forehand) for both right and left-handed guns.

The reason that I am covering this special variant is that you must use the technique covered in Lesson Fourteen - the diagonal swing.

A RIGHT-HANDED GUN'S
HIGH FOREHAND SWING

First, the right-handed gun's forehand swing (the bird coming from the right and passing to the left). Wait in the ready position with your weight on your front foot (left foot). Lift your right heel so that your body weight preferably is really on your left foot. Angle your pelvis so that your upper body is leaning while the left shoulder rises and right shoulder is lowered. The rib is now angled in relation to the ground plane - and - the barrels will follow the target's diagonal line of flight. By moving your hip to the left, leaning your upper body and lifting your left shoulder accordingly, you can now swing from the starting point behind the bird and past it simply by rotating your upper body. You do not need to use your arms to help lift the barrels. If you think about this, you will discover that you are swinging in exactly the same way as when you swing

parallel to the ground. However, with the difference that your upper body is leaning and the swing is angled upwards in relation to the ground plane.

THE LEFT-HANDED GUN'S
HIGH FOREHAND SWING

Now to the left-handed gun's forehand swing (the bird coming from the left and passing to the right). Wait in the ready position with your weight on your front foot (right foot). Lift your left heel so that your body weight preferably is really on your right foot. Angle your pelvis so that your upper body is leaning while the right shoulder rises and the left shoulder is lowered. The rib is now angled in relation to the ground plane - and - the barrels will follow the target's diagonal line of flight. By moving your hip to the right, leaning your upper body and lifting your right shoulder accordingly, you can now swing from the starting point behind the bird and past it simply by rotating your upper body. You do not need to use your arms to help lift the barrels. If you think about this, you will discover that you are swinging in exactly the same way as when you swing parallel to the ground. However, with the difference that your upper body is leaning and the swing is angled upwards in relation to the ground plane.

Now for the most common mistake. If you shoot with your shoulder area at a right angle to the ground plane, you have to lift the shotgun continuously with your front hand so that the barrels follow the direction of flight and pass through the target. You will meet resistance from your trunk. Another effect of this swing error is that you perhaps cannot follow through properly at the end of the swing. The muzzles drop and you shoot under.

When you have tried this swing until you have no problems with it, then it's time to change position and swing to the other direction.

THE RIGHT-HANDED GUN'S
HIGH BACKHAND SWING

The bird will pass to the right. The right-handed gun leans the upper body to the left and lifts the right shoulder accordingly. The ribcage leans so that the swing is diagonal and again follows parallel with the bird's line of flight. Wait in the ready position. Mount behind the bird as before, swing through and pull the trigger when the muzzles pass the target. Despite the mount and swing being perfect, there nevertheless is resistance. You can facilitate the swing and swing further out to the right if you allow your body weight to rest on the outside of your right foot and let its inside leave contact with the ground while you turn your right knee in at the same time. How much resistance is felt naturally depends on both age and flexibility. However, you can never swing as far to the right as to the left. You just have to accept this.

THE LEFT-HANDED GUN'S
HIGH BACKHAND SWING

The bird will pass to the left. The left-handed gun leans the upper body to the left and lifts the left shoulder accordingly. The ribcage leans so that the swing is diagonal and follows parallel with the bird's line of flight. Wait in the ready position. Mount behind the bird as before, swing through and pull the trigger when the muzzles pass the target. Despite the mount and swing being perfect, there nevertheless is resistance. You can facilitate the swing and swing further out to the left if you allow your body weight to rest on the outside of your left foot and let the inside leave contact with the ground while you turn your left knee in at the same time. How much resistance is felt naturally depends on both age and flexibility. However, you can never swing as far to the left as to the right. You just have to accept this.

POINTS TO OBSERVE:

When it meets resistance, the body prefers to cheat and make things easier, and this causes mistakes.

In order to compensate for resistance once it begins, it is easy to start by rolling with your upper body. The barrels lower to under the bird's line of flight. The result in nine cases out of ten is that you miss under and behind. In addition to the rolling, many people want to help the swing by moving the shotgun with their arms - that is by moving the aimed right angle to the target laterally. The swing stops and the shot inevitably passes behind the target.

A SUMMARY FOR WHEN YOU
ARE SHOOTING THESE TARGETS:

1. Check that your feet are in the correct position. This is very important. A good swing starts with your feet. If you are standing with legs apart and locking up with subsequent movements, then most of what you do will be absolutely wrong.
2. Check that you have the right starting position.
3. Focus on the target.
4. Starting point: Mount on the point where you first saw the bird and move the shotgun calmly forwards and upwards with your front hand so that the stock slides into the correct position against your shoulder, and turn your head (without tilting) so that the comb is in contact with your cheek at the height of the upper row of your teeth.
5. Focus the entire time on the target and nothing else.
6. Swing through the target.
7. Pull the trigger when the muzzles pass the target.
8. The subsequent delay will result in the correct lead.
9. The actual shot is fired.
10. Continue with the swing through.

As always - you should practise this as often as possible in your living room. Position yourself near the wall, mount on the ceiling moulding in the corner, swing in parallel to the ceiling moulding and pull the trigger when you reach the wall. You will quickly discover the importance of a correct placement of your feet and that your upper body must have the correct angle in relation to the line of flight (ceiling moulding). The ribcage should follow the line of flight without you needing to roll your upper body or use your arms to help you swing the shotgun. The swing should come from below at your feet and hips.

Summary - Your shoulders must always be angled so that your shoulder area is parallel with the target's line of flight.

At times one is struck...

... by a wizard-wheeze. As when training pointers for partridge shooting, for example, and one lives in the middle of a forest. What do you do when the only bird available is a hazel hen?

A while ago, I had been given several carrier pigeons, about twenty, donated by an enthusiast who was in the process of quitting the hobby. The pigeons sat in their new loft cooing. One pleasant characteristic of carrier pigeons is that they always try to fly home from wherever you release them. But to what purpose? The Royal Mail, as it was called in that time, is quicker and more effective. It was then that the idea came. Why not place the pigeons in wire cages with spring locks and release mechanisms? No sooner said than done. The cages were made and release mechanisms constructed with the help of old mousetraps.

A bird is a bird to a pointer, I reasoned to myself. The pigeons were placed out in nearby fields already at daybreak. They sat there until late afternoon when the pointers were trained. They found the caged pigeons immediately. They stood transfixed. They then advanced gently while I searched for the release mechanisms at the same time as I tried to train one dog to back the other. The tendency to rush in was controlled and everything was fine. I was happy with the pointers' incredible ability to find the birds until I understood that it was not the birds they found. They were following my scent leftover from the morning when I had set out the cages.

The project was abandoned but it had one good result, I think. The way in which the pointers covered the ground was affected in that their beats became irregular. In this way, they became more skilled in finding well-concealed birds under confusing scent conditions. They became game finders however instead of just game searchers. Not always ideal under normal shooting conditions, but of great benefit when game is scarce. Every cloud has a silver lining.

LESSON TWENTY-THREE
SHOOTING GOING AWAY TARGETS

Shooting going away targets is carried out in exactly the same way as all other shots, except that the angles are much smaller and you come in much closer to the target to begin with. Even though the angles are small, it is important to first focus on the bird, mount behind, find your starting point, accelerate the swing, swing past and pull the trigger when the muzzles pass the target.

Before you start, by way of introduction I would like to emphasis two important things: One - how you hold the shotgun in the ready position. Two - body posture. I covered this in Lesson Fifteen, but I'll repeat it here.

In the ready position, you must always make sure that the barrels are pointed parallel to the ground. From there, you lean upwards when mounting and firing. If you hold the barrels aimed up at a 45-degree angle, you must quickly lower them for mounting. The movement is very expansive and there is a major risk that you will lose control of the barrels.

If the barrels are pointing diagonally down to the side, then they may be aimed at a dog in front of you. An accidental shot in this position would easily be fatal for the dog. Consequently, make sure that the barrels are aimed parallel with the ground, but over the dogs, when you adopt the ready position.

When shooting going away targets, it is important that your body weight is moved firmly forward on your front foot. While mounting, you lean forwards so that the shotgun is at a 45-degree angle in relation to your upper body. You do a "Skalman" as I described in Lesson Fifteen. In addition, it is especially important that you really lean forward with both the shotgun and your body. Imagine that you have a bayonet fixed onto the muzzles and that you are stabbing it through the target.

When you practise shooting going away targets, there are several things you should watch out for.

You make quite small movements with the shotgun when shooting going away targets. Despite this, you have to push your body firmly forward during mounting. The mount then is correct and you can swing through the target correctly. If you don't lean forward but instead mount in a more upright position, you will be in the wrong position right from the start. You won't be able to put the whole act of mounting together properly.

Another aspect that arises when shooting going away quarry is stress. The bird is flying away from you and you think

it's going to fly out of range. The mistake that many people make is to mount directly on the target. The starting point is wrong then and the swing has no speed. The lead won't be right then either.

A third mistake, also caused by stress, is that you fail to transfer your body weight to the front foot and mount the gun predominantly through the forend. Pay attention to whether you mount upright and lay the shotgun towards your cheek with your front hand. This mount is completely wrong (see Lesson Four) and the likelihood of you hitting the target becomes very small. So, take the steps in their correct order again: Firmly forward with your weight on your front foot. Lean your upper body forwards so that the heel comes into your shoulder correctly and so that the entire butt is in contact with your shoulder. Move your head forward and lift it so that the comb is in contact with your cheek at a height level with the upper row of your teeth. Don't tilt your head, just turn it slightly to make contact.

Accordingly, take it calmly when shooting going away quarry. You have plenty of time. As always - practise dry runs with mounting on low targets at home in the living room. Practice makes perfect!

Summary - Despite the angles being small when shooting going away targets, the technique is the same as with all other shot angles. Starting point. Swing through. Pull the trigger when the barrels pass through the target.

Shredded grouse

INGREDIENTS FOR 4 PORTIONS

4 x grouse breast cut into centimetre wide thin strips
4 dl funnel chanterelles
2 x medium sized finely chopped shallots
Butter
4 dl cream
Salt and pepper
Finely chopped parsley

COOKING PROCESS
Heat up a large cast iron pan
Heat the butter, shallots, chanterelles and grouse
so that everything is coloured.
Add the cream and simmer quickly together
(the grouse should be pink inside)
Add salt and pepper

Serve with potato cake or as a first course on toast.
Sprinkle over the parsley when serving

LESSON TWENTY-FOUR
SHOOTING GROUND TARGETS

When you shoot ground targets, it's important that you really lean forwards exactly as you do when shooting low going away targets. See the previous lesson for a review if needed.

When you shoot ground targets, you don't need to think about leaning your upper body to the side to find the line. Here you mount with your shoulders parallel with the ground and swing straight out to the sides.

Otherwise, the swing is exactly the same as when you practise different shooting angles against flying targets. You mount behind the target, accelerate through the target and pull the trigger when the barrels pass the target.

If you have access to a sporting range with clay rabbit throwers, you can practise the same shots as with game shooting - angled incoming, crossing shots left and right as well as going away shots at different angles.

The mistakes you make naturally are the same as in the previous lessons. If you miss, you can seek guidance there and correct your mistakes.

Summary - Same start, same accelerating swing and same firing as in all shooting angles.

Note:
When shooting deer with a shotgun, it is very important to not shoot with a swing that is too fast. Make sure that the mount is perfect and that the swing is more "following" than leading and accelerating. On the other hand, shots against a fast hare should be fired with a speedy swing. Unfortunately, shots at deer that only maim are the result of the gun lifting the head for a better view of the target and the shotgun accordingly shooting high.

APPENDIX 1
FITTING THE STOCK

If you have a well-adjusted stock, the barrels and rib will be centred under your eye. If you check the direction of the barrels, you will notice that they point in the direction in which you are looking. This is the reason why you don't need to aim or check. You instinctively know and sense the direction in which the barrels are aimed. The result is that you can focus on the target the whole time.

I stated initially that it is enough if the shotgun suits you "reasonably" well when you start seriously training for game shooting. What I mean by "reasonable" is that your eye is centred over the rib when you mount. This is sufficient because even if you follow the instructions for mounting to the letter, you nevertheless in the beginning will mount slightly differently each time.

Here's a "hypothetical" experiment to help clarify this. Imagine you had a laser sight built into the barrels, and that the laser beam could be directed as a point against a cross 20 metres away with each point recorded for each mounting. As a beginner, you would quickly discover that you never mount on the same spot each time. After several thousand mountings, there should be several thousand points around the cross and within a circle that is quite large in the beginning.

What would happen now if a beginner shoots at a moving target, a wild duck for example, at a distance of 20 metres with such a deviation when mounting? From earlier lessons you know that you should pull the trigger when the barrels swing past the bill. But where are they pointing in reality? The aim entirely depends on how they pointed when you mount behind the target. For this reason the answer is obvious. They can point over, under, slightly in front of, slightly behind OR in the centre of the target. A beginner never has perfect control

of the direction - but - despite this, can hit the bird at this shooting distance. Several hits will be very good, others a little worse, but on the whole, the hits will be quite acceptable.

If such a record were kept, you would also quickly discover the results of continuous mounting training. The points would be collected within an increasingly narrower circle. The mountings would become increasingly similar. The hits would become increasingly better. This is one side of the coin. The other is that the centre of the circle would unerringly be slightly over, under or at the side of the exact spot you are trying to aim at. It is then, if not before, that you make maximum gains by adjusting the stock according to your personal dimensions. As I pointed out, it is the stock that aims - not you!

Determining the correct stock dimensions requires consulting a shooting instructor who can check your mounting and who has access to a try gun with an adjustable stock. Following adjustments, the shooting instructor can read the settings. You then submit these dimensions to a stock maker, who makes the stock adjustments required.

If you have worked through all of the lessons in this book, you are without doubt ready for further "hypothetical" experiments. If you could perform the same tests that I have described here above, you would discover that mountings following a stock adjustment lie more evenly and closely collected around the mount point. Note that when you have reached this far in your shooting training, the stock dimensions should be checked every third or fourth year. We human beings change throughout our entire lives!

Time for yet another "hypothetical" experiment. Imagine that the accuracy of your mounts at a distance of 20 metres is such that they fall within a circle having a diameter of 30 centimetres. As you now know, and as I hope you are now convinced, you should never aim! This is a "hypothetical"

experiment. Nothing else. Such accuracy for mounting is acceptable in the beginning. But what happens if you move the shooting distance out to 35 metres? The circle really grows. The aim no longer would be acceptable. With a moving target, you would miss or have predominantly poor hits, even if the mounting and swing were perfect otherwise! You can easily check this assertion yourself. Try to shoot a longer distance than normal on a clay pigeon shooting range. You will discover that even if you have good kills at short distances, your misses and poor hits increase markedly when the distance grows. This calls for careful consideration when hunting live quarry. Never overestimate your capacity by shooting at a distance farther than your ability permits.

IT IS IMPORTANT THAT YOU KNOW YOUR OWN CAPACITY AND ADJUST ACCORDINGLY!

When you start shooting live quarry, you must unconditionally decide the maximum distance that you can shoot in with good results, and never shoot beyond this, however tempting it may be. How you judge distance is discussed in Lesson Seventeen. There is an ethical aspect here that you can never ignore. If you shoot at a distance beyond your capacity, the likelihood is that you will maim your quarry. You will cause unnecessary suffering to the game, and perhaps a slow and painful death. Game shooting is more than "just a pleasant past-time," you in fact shoulder a great responsibility!

AMMUNITION, TIGHT CHOKES AND SHOT

A constantly recurring question: Which choke is best and which shot sizes should be chosen for different game?

It's a question of taste, but...

If we start with the choke, there is no general answer for what you should choose for a hunting weapon. Normal chokes are:

- Improved cylinder/Quarter
- Quarter/Half
- Quarter/Three-quarters
- Half/Full

As I mentioned, the combination you choose is a question of taste. With game shooting and a shooting distance of around 20 metres, one of the more open combinations is highly preferable. Quarter / Half is an excellent choice, for example.

More important than the type of choke is how the shot is distributed within the shot pattern. The more even the distribution, the better. "Even" here means that the distance between the pellets should be approximately the same throughout the entire shot pattern. An even shot pattern accordingly is free from stray collections of shot and conversely, large gaps. A good method for studying the distribution of the shot is to shoot at a sheet of paper about the size of a square metre at a distance of 15 metres.

How the shot is distributed within the shot pattern does not just depend on how the barrels have been machined. The ammunition is also significant. For this reason, it is a good idea to test shoot the shotgun with different types of ammunition from different manufacturers. The choice is simple. Choose the ammunition that gives the best and most even distribution.

When it comes to the choice of shot size for different types of game, it is simplest to follow the recommendations of the ammunition manufacturers. They are based on trials and many years of experience.

LOAD WEIGHTS

I really don't have any views on this either. Well, perhaps one ... choose the loading the shotgun is designed for. If you choose heavy loadings for a good old side-by-side, this means that you are unnecessarily subjecting the weapon to great stress. Over and under type shotguns are less sensitive in this regard. One question you could ask in this connection is whether it really is necessary to be at the limit of the shotgun's capacity. Most often it is not. The hit is more important than the number of pellets in the cartridge and the size of the powder charge.

MYTHS

There are a number of myths surrounding tightly choked shotguns and shot sizes. One is that you can shoot longer distances with a significantly tight choked shotgun. Another is that large shot kills "better."

Let us examine both of these myths a little more closely.

Being able to shoot a longer distance with a significantly tight choked shotgun does contain a grain of truth. The question that should then be asked is whether you are capable of shooting at the limit of the shotgun's range. In this book we have agreed, I hope, that small errors in mounting and swing become exaggerated the longer the shooting distance. The hits will be poorer and as a consequence, there will be more maiming shots. We have also arrived at this conclusion: You should never shoot at distances that exceed your own capacity.

That large shot kills "better" must evidently be wrong. A charge of shot does not kill by means of injury to the game's inner organs. It is the shock that kills. That is, the effect a lot of shot has when hitting the target at the same point in time.

There is another aspect of large shot that I find distinctly distasteful. From what I understand, guns who are insistent about large shot sizes are really trying to compensate for poor hits. With a poor hit, the shot wounds and the bird continues to fly because the shot that hit it is too sparse. To use fewer and larger shot worsens this type of situation.

To summarise. Shooting practice is more important than considerations regarding weapon design and ballistics. A few lessons now and then together with an experienced shooting instructor will always results in better hits, and accordingly, improve results on the hunting field.

It's as simple as that.

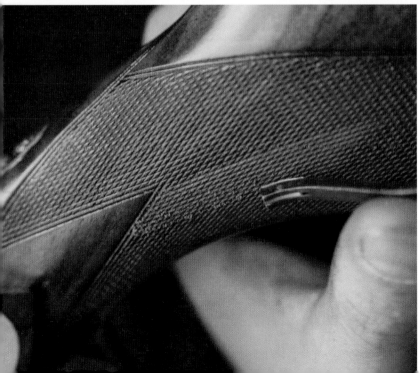

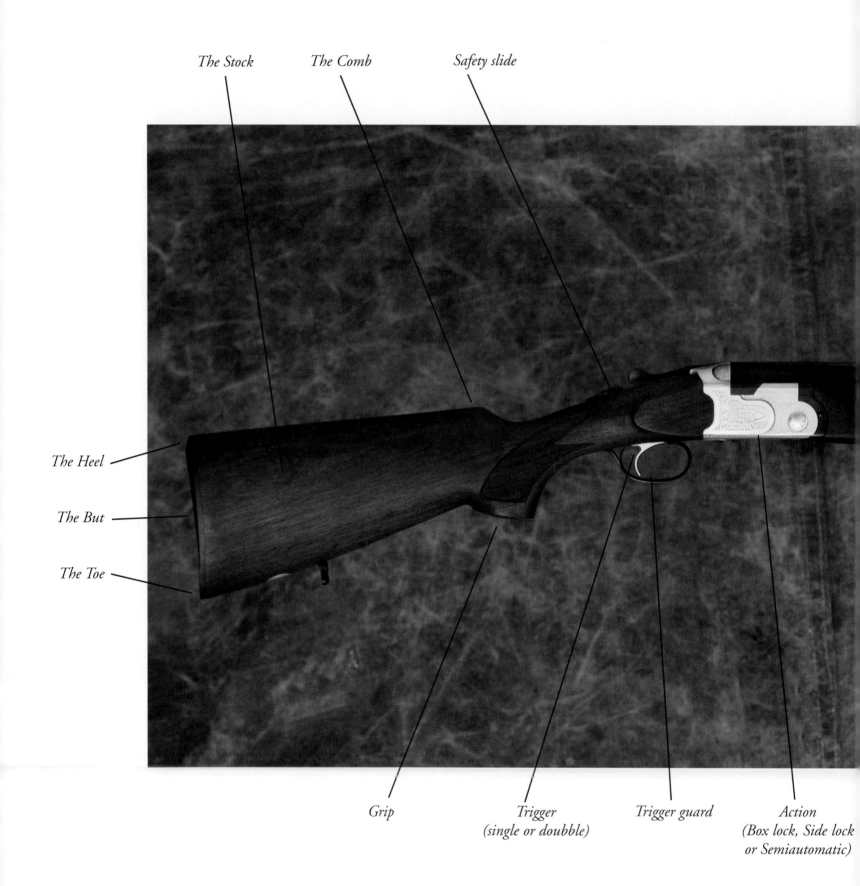

The Stock   The Comb   Safety slide

The Heel

The But

The Toe

Grip   Trigger
(single or doubble)   Trigger guard   Action
(Box lock, Side lock
or Semiautomatic)

Forend   Top rib   Barrels (Side by side   Sight
                                  or Over and under)

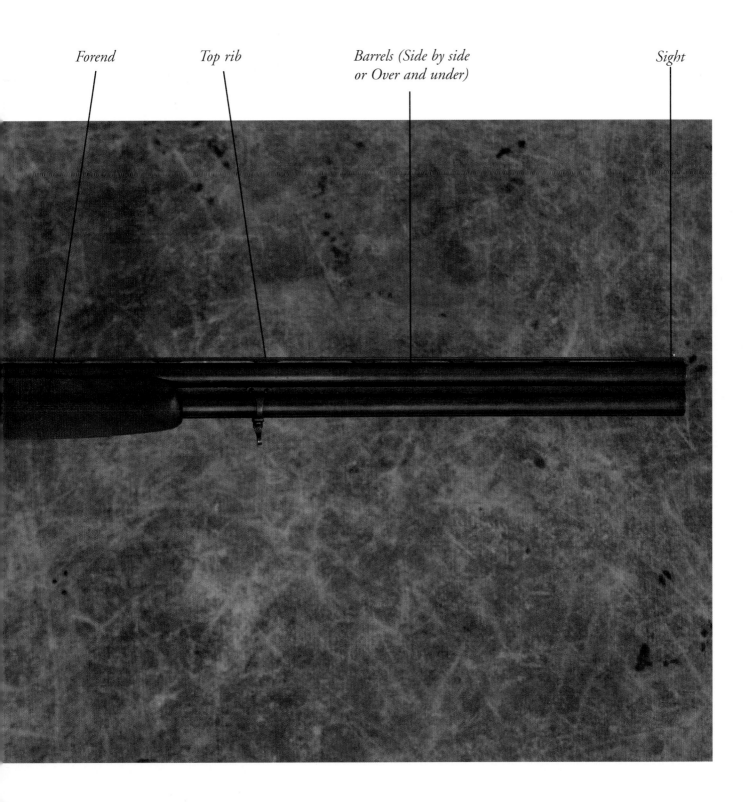

A natural pattern of movement is easy to repeat.
It is also graceful and harmonious, and it results in
the good timing that is so essential for successful shotgun shooting.
It is so obvious and timeless that it is rarely documented,
even if there is an advocate such as Tom.

PL